SPY
SCHOOL

—

ARE YOU
SHARP ENOUGH
TO BE A
KGB AGENT?

ST. MARTIN'S PRESS
NEW YORK

www.stmartins.com

Published by agreement with Kontext Agency, Sweden
Translated from Russian by Svetlana Shcholokova

Designed by Marcia Mihotich

The Library of Congress Cataloging-in-Publication Data
is available upon request.

ISBN 978-1-250-19998-0 (hardcover)
ISBN 978-1-250-19999-7 (ebook)

Our books may be purchased in bulk for promotional, educational, or business use. Please contact your local bookseller or the Macmillan Corporate and Premium Sales Department at 1-800-221-7945, extension 5442, or by email at MacmillanSpecialMarkets@macmillan.com.

First published in Russia by OOO Alpina Publisher

Previously published in the United Kingdom by Boxtree, an imprint of Pan Macmillan

First U.S. Edition: September 2018

10   9   8   7   6   5   4   3   2   1

Contents

INTRODUCTION

Congratulations. If you are reading this document, you have been accepted for a place at Spy School.

When most people think of the word spy, they imagine gadgets – laser pens and exploding cigarette lighters – but the most important piece of equipment an agent has is their brain. Memory is vital to the work of an agent. The need for total secrecy often prevents them from recording anything, so operatives have to rely on their brains to retain and reproduce an incredible amount of information with absolute accuracy.

Over the coming pages, we will teach you how to enhance your memory and sharpen your mind with a range of exercises developed over many years and used to train top Russian intelligence agents.*

Real intelligence, not the kind we see in films, is about working with information. Reconstructing the whole picture from tiny fragments of information – that is the task of an intelligence agent and this is what you test yourself against here at Spy School. You will develop skills tested in the most extreme of environments and unlock the full capability of your brain.

---

* Although all the characters appearing in this work are fictional, and any resemblance to real persons is purely coincidental, the events described in the book are based on a true story. It is also necessary to state here that all the data provided in this book is taken from public sources.

Structure of the book

The book is divided into chapters corresponding to the progress of an agent through their career. You will pass all stages of the intelligence school, from a junior operative to a double agent, from the simplest work to the most dangerous and complex.

You will follow the story of a counter-intelligence operation, told through a series of documents and the diary entries of its main character placed throughout the book. You will be asked questions about this story, so while reading, try to remember as much as you can.

Each stage contains instructions on memory formation procedures and practice exercises. The exercises from the first stages may seem easy, but they get harder later on. Try to learn the techniques and methods connected to the first simple tasks. Even if you can do the tasks without using the prescribed techniques, the problems will get harder later on, so try to use them from the beginning. Shortcuts taken early on will slow your progress later in the programme.

There are two types of exercise in this book. The first are interactive and it's best to perform them immediately while reading the book, repeating them several times to ensure you learn them. Track your progress in the notes sections throughout.

If you can't do all of an exercise, return to the techniques for which the exercise is designed. Re-read them and do the less complex version of the exercise several times. For the second type of exercise it's not necessary to have the book in front of you. You can do them in a variety of situations: while on holiday, queuing at a supermarket or while travelling to work . . .

Don't worry if you can't complete a task on the first try. You will learn most when you stretch yourself to your limits. The brain is like a muscle and most of us have become accustomed to using only a very small part of its capacity. You need to build up the strength of your brain through exercising it. Stick at it and you, and others around you, are sure to notice your progress.

In addition to techniques, instructions, exercises and tasks, the book also includes facts about human attention, imagination and memory, as well as how to work with them.

A SCUFFLE BEFORE THE ELECTIONS

A series of unusual events took place in Buenos Aires on 10 December 1954 during a pre-election meeting between voters and Argentina's Peronist candidate Garcia Pughese. As is usual for such events, it opened with a candidate's introductory speech, but ended in a mass brawl. Pughese's calls for a confrontation with the Socialists were taken literally. The approximately 300 attendees who exited the cinema where the meeting was held began chanting slogans and headed to the Socialists' election headquarters. An aggressive mob, armed with garden tools, stones and sticks, broke windows, furniture and beat up people. Several party representatives were hospitalized, including the Socialist candidate Gabriel Acritiso.

There was not much police interference in the fighting, bar the short-term detention of several people. It is notable that the detainees denied their participation in the brawl, but could not explain why they had been arrested and claimed they had come to the election meeting out of curiosity. The fight itself seemed like a mass psychosis, beginning unexpectedly and ending suddenly. Observers rate the Peronist Party's chance of being elected as high. The strength of its support hasn't been diminished, even by the recent rumours that the election campaign is supported by German consultants, who had served the fascist regime in Germany and escaped from Europe after the defeat of the Third Reich in the spring of 1945.

12. December 1954

The year is ending. I'm trying to take a good look back at it and see what it was like. Except for the Spanish, I can only describe it as boring. I really only started learning Spanish because I was bored — something to keep myself busy. I'm tired of academic psychology. Working in the dean's office is boring. My personal life hasn't changed.

I should have got into graduate school. Maybe I should try again next year?

[Extract from the journal of Andrei Simanov]

CONFIDENTIAL

15 December 1954

Director of the Second Department
USSR KGB

In accordance with the KGB act 'On replacing
operational employees without necessary background
who do not fulfil an assignment' of 1 December 1954,
and with the goal of strengthening the undercover
unit among academic and artistic intelligentsia,
agent recruitment preparation among the MSU staff was
conducted. I request authorization to recruit the
following people:

1. Evgeny Petrovich Ivanov, b. 1931;

2. Elena Vassilyevna Ilyina, b. 1929;

3. Andrei Nikolaevich Simonov, b. 1930.

Operational profiles on the above persons are
included.

Deputy Chief of the Ninth Division
of the Second Main Directorate
Lieutenant Colonel N. V. Ilyin

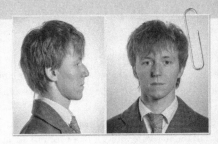

5 December 1954,
Moscow

OPERATIONAL PROFILE
Simonov, Andrei Nikolaevich

Andrei Simonov was born in Leningrad in 1930.

Father — Simonov, Nikolai Matveevich, b. 1902, labourer.Currently
a mechanic on the steam tug Miner in Leningrad seaport. Was
exempted from military service on the front.

Mother — Simonova (née Ivanova), Olga, b. 1910, labourer.
Currently a crane operator in the Leningrad seaport.

Studied at high school No. 120 in Leningrad. After graduating in
1948, entered the Moscow State University, Psychology Section
of the Philosophy Department. Graduated in 1953 with honours
and received a reference for postgraduate study. Thesis on 'The
Psychophysiological Methods of Establishing the Truthfulness of
the Investigative and Court Testimony' was written under the
guidance of Professor A. R. Luria.

Postgraduate study and writing activities were postponed for
research and practical experience. Currently employed as a
secretary in the dean's office of the Philosophy Department. Member
of the Young Communist League. MSU instructors consider him a
promising specialist. His decision not to enter postgraduate study
immediately was met with understanding.

Simonov's connections with instructors and students in the
Psychology Section of the Philosophy Department are of interest to
the KGB. In the future, Simonov will develop more opportunities
to gain information. Has good capabilities: high intelligence,
good memory. Calm. Emotionally stable. No social problems. Speaks
German. Plays sports. Attends football matches.

Interested in psychophysiology, hypnosis and social psychology.

Not married.

Expectation of recruitment on an ideological and political basis.

Deputy Chief of the Ninth Division
of the Second Main Directorate
Lieutenant Colonel N. V. Ilyin

Memory capacity

People don't take full advantage of their memories' capabilities. Moreover, very few people even know the extent of these capabilities.

A few examples. After only one visit, Russian painter Nikolai Ge reproduced in detail the baroque interior of a room in 'Mon Plaisir' palace.

Mozart could write down a complex score after listening to a piece of music only once. Having once heard Gregorio Allegri's 'Miserere', which had been kept secret by the Vatican up until that point, he was able to bring it into the public domain. Mozart was fourteen years old at the time.

Winston Churchill knew almost all of Shakespeare's works by heart. He used them to practise his oratory.

In 1960, Hungarian chess player Janos Flash played fifty-two games simultaneously without looking at any of the boards. At the end of the game, which lasted more than thirteen hours, Flash remembered all the moves on all fifty-two boards.

But it's not just celebrated geniuses who have outstanding memories. In one experiment, ordinary people were shown 10,000 slides, and then tested on how many they could remember. It was found that their image recognition was about 80% accurate. When the images chosen for the experiment were unusual, bright or colourful, accuracy increased to almost 100%.

From this we can see that:

1. The main problem of human memory is not remembering information, but recalling and reproducing it when it's needed. Every person has the makings of a great memory. To develop it, you need to master a number of techniques;

2. The human brain is very good at remembering images. Therefore, most techniques for memorizing information – mnemonics – are based on using our imagination to transfer abstract verbal and numerical information into images.

Test Yourself

In what year was Andrei Nikolaevich Simonov born?

A) 1929

B) 1930

C) 1932

D) 1928

Types of memory

Modern psychology identifies three types of memory: sensory, short-term and long-term.

Sensory memory stores information perceived directly by the senses: what we see, hear, feel, smell and taste after the original stimulus has ceased. Sensory memory is short and allows individuals to retain impressions of sensory information for no more than half a second. But sensory memory is very important, because everything that connects us to our environment passes through it. It is thanks to sensory memory that we perceive a sequence of short, single pictures in the cinema as a continuous movement.

Information that deserves attention goes from sensory memory into short-term memory, where it can be stored for several minutes or hours. Short-term memory is used, for example, when we silently repeat to ourselves a phone number while searching for a pen and paper to write it down.

Important information goes from short-term memory into long-term memory, where it can be stored for years. Typically, the process of long-term storage of information occurs unconsciously. That is why we often forget the important things and remember minor details that should have been forgotten long ago. However, there are methods that can be used to develop the conscious storage of long-term information.

This book will help you to develop both your short- and long-term memory, and learn how to consciously transfer information from short-term memory into long-term.

A successful spy must have the ability to notice important details in what they see and hear, and also to reinterpret that information, linking it with what they already know. In other words, the kind of memory we are looking to develop requires the attention to notice things and the imagination to connect them to what we already know. This is where our programme begins.

Attention and memory

Attention is the ability to perceive information selectively, to see and to hear what is needed, ignoring distractions. Noise does not prevent a person who is concentrating from being able to read. They perceive the text, ignoring extraneous sounds. Concentration allows you to focus on the nuances and details of what you need to remember without overloading your brain by paying attention to everything equally.

Trained attention differs from weak attention, because training allows attention to be directed. You are able to focus quickly, hold your attention on one thing for a long time when necessary, and easily redirect it when you change activities.

Exercise

Focusing your attention on one thing for a long time is not as easy as you might think. Try examining something you have in front of you. For example, a wristwatch. Examine every detail. Inspect each division on the dial, every scratch on its face. Have you examined everything? Keep on looking, try to find something new.

After a few minutes, it will be hard for you to focus on the watch. Suddenly you will notice that you are not thinking about the watch and that associations have led your thoughts elsewhere. For example, you were looking at the watch, trying to concentrate. Then, you saw the number 11 and remembered an important meeting at 11:00 a.m. Then your thoughts went to your colleague who was also attending the meeting, then to a book the colleague told you about, then . . . You forgot about the watch. Can you reverse this journey? Remember how you got from the watch to what you were thinking about. Go back through the chain of associations to the watch and keep on examining it. Remember what you thought about the book that belongs to the colleague, and then about the colleague, then about the meeting that you have to attend, then about the meeting time - 11:00 a.m. Remember that it is the time associated with the number 11 on the dial and that the dial is connected to the watch.

By walking back along the road of associations, this exercise allows you to develop the ability to direct your attention.

Test yourself

Voters broke into the headquarters of which
political movement?

A) Anarchists

B) Communists

C) Socialists

D) Peronists

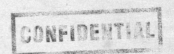

No. 67s

17 December 1954,
Moscow

Authorization to recruit Andrei Nikolaevich Simonov
(b. 1930) granted.

Test the agent for work as a CHIS.

Head of Second Main Directorate
KGB of the USSR
Lieutenant General P. V. Fedotov

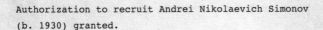

Attention span, the '7 ± 2' rule

One of the main features of attention is that the number of objects (words, numbers, items or ideas) an average person can hold in working memory is somewhere between five and nine.

It is almost impossible to exceed this number, but there are some ways to get round the restriction. All it takes is grouping the data into blocks. For example, the telephone number +74957894179 contains twelve items of information, and after grouping it into +7 (495) 789 41 79, there are only five. And these five can be compressed to four, if you know that +7 (495) means Moscow, Russia.

These 5–9 units need to be used to 100% of their capacity. This memory training programme will help you to improve your attention. Follow the instructions, practise regularly, and the result will not be long in coming. Remember the quote from the Disciplinary Code of the Soviet Military: 'The soldier must endure steadfastly and courageously all the hardships and privations of military service.'

Exercise

Performing two tasks at once improves your ability to switch attention. Read two books, alternating a paragraph from each. Switching the radio station every few seconds, listen to two news programmes simultaneously (as you do this, try to reconstruct any missing pieces of information through context). Watch two TV programmes.

Don't get carried away! The simultaneous execution of multiple tasks is good as an exercise for training the attention, but it is not an effective way to successfully complete a large number of tasks at once.

★ Train your brain – Schulte Tables, 5×5

Schulte Tables can help speed the development of mental perception, including peripheral vision and attention, self-control and the ability to focus.

On this page is a table containing 5 columns and 5 rows. Numbers from 1 to 25 are randomly arranged in the cells. Your task is to find the numbers in order.

Do not move your eyes from cell to cell and do not say the numbers out loud or to yourself. Fix your sight on the centre of the table and use only your peripheral vision to search for the numbers. This will be hard at first – don't give up. Later on, this skill will help you with a variety of tasks, ranging from observation to speed reading.

Come back to this exercise often. Over time, you will learn to visualize the table in your mind. With training, the time can be reduced to 12–15 seconds or even less.

20	2	16	9	18
12	24	17	14	1
19	21	10	15	5
22	4	8	3	23
25	13	7	6	11

19 December 1954

Long day. Finals are around the corner: the dean's
office is manic, so are the students and instructors. And
there's a huge pile of papers.

In the evening, when I was coming home, the KGb
tried to recruit me. Before I knew it, I was having a
conversation with a passenger, a normal-looking academic
type, short, chubby, in a grey trench coat.

Suddenly, he addresses me by name and says, 'Would
you like to help us?' When I realized exactly who the
grey trench was suggesting I help, I refused right away.
But somehow, he managed to turn me back to the
question. He wasn't cajoling, threatening or manipulating
me. The work, he says, will help me practise what I
learned in university. 'We need good psychologists,' he
said. On top of that, I'm being recruited into counter-
intelligence: catching foreign spies seems like meaningful
work to me. More meaningful than the same experiments
and surveys day after day, and way more meaningful
than paperwork at the dean's office. In the end, I
promised to think about it, and the grey trench promised
to be in touch.

In parting, he asked me not to tell anyone of our
conversation. And not to leave any records of him. But
I didn't follow his instructions there. I guess there's
something of the spy in me after all, as no one has
seen this journal in the ten years I've been writing it.

Tricks with attention

Any productive person must be able to control his or her attention. But there are also ways to control others' attention. After all, if you control a person's attention, you can control them.

Attention can be compared to a spotlight in the darkness: we only see the illuminated portion. Redirecting our interlocutor's attention, we can show him what we want and hide what we do not want him to see. All magic tricks and stunts are based on the skill of shifting a viewer's attention. For this purpose, a magician uses distracting motions, bright ribbons, scarves, flares and explosions.

Intelligence officers, who often have to work under the surveillance of external counter-intelligence, act almost the same way. While being searched, an intelligence agent casually asked a police officer to hold a package of napkins. The officers searched her bag thoroughly and found nothing suspicious. The secret documents she was carrying were tucked between the napkins.

Another good trick is to stretch the hidden action in time, expanding it into several stages, each of which will seem completely innocuous. For example, to pick up an object unnoticed, you can stop in front of it, open your bag, take out your gloves, drop one of them, lean over the glove, drop a handkerchief, pick up the object and the glove and go away, leaving the handkerchief lying on the ground. Surveillance will notice that you dropped and picked up some objects. The attention of observers will be drawn to your handkerchief, and your clumsiness will not cause suspicion. No one will notice the number of objects you dropped, or which ones you picked up.

Another example of 'stretching' an action is transferring a notebook to someone in a cafe without being noticed. You come over and take out a notebook from your briefcase. Then you talk, open the notebook, write something down, put it down nearby and keep talking. Then you get up, put gloves on the table, put on your coat, pick up your gloves and leave. Your notebook is left on the table, and your companion will take it when they finish their coffee and leave.

NON-DISCLOSURE AGREEMENT
WITH STATE SECURITY BODIES

I, Simonov, Andrei Nikolaevich, of my own free will
agree to cooperate with state security bodies. I
undertake to fulfil in good faith the operational
assignments I receive, to keep my work a secret, to
maintain confidentiality, and not to disclose any
information obtained in the course of my work.

A. N. Simonov,
19 December 1954

20 December 1954,
Moscow

Assign agent A. N. Simonov (1930) the code
name 'Simonides'. Admit him to the accelerated
intelligence course.

                        Deputy Chief of the
                        Ninth Division of the
                        Second Main Directorate
                    Lieutenant Colonel N. V. Ilyin

Working memory

In addition to sensory, short-term and long-term memory, there is also a separate category called working memory. It stores data for immediate processing. The main distinction of working memory is that everything contained in it will be erased immediately after switching to another task.

Recent studies have established a close connection between working memory capacity and intelligence level. It is obvious that the more data a person can store in working memory, the higher that person's ability to notice relationships and create new knowledge, which are the abilities measured by an IQ test. Moreover, the capacity of working memory is related to attention. The higher it is, the more objects the person can hold in their attention simultaneously.

It is notable that the average person's working memory capacity is that same size of somewhere between five and nine. Those whose number is smaller have more trouble controlling their attention and organizing their behaviour.

To find out the capacity of your working memory, memorize the numbers from the list below one by one and write them down on a piece of paper. Do not group the numbers in pairs, triples, etc. For example, represent 1234 as 'one-two-three-four', and not as 'twelve thirty-four'. When you reach the end of the list, count how many digits there are in the last number you recorded correctly. This will be the capacity of your working memory.

850	708243	8203947529
834	0972435	3982775235
4399	8931432	06016554392
9543	43249034	61085082684
82140	24349328	010178844818
38587	905298713	768582301939
932435	378072043	

★ Train your Brain – Pairs 4×3

Take a pack of cards. Count a sequence of six cards from any two suits – for example A, 2, 3, 4, 5, 6 hearts and A, 2, 3, 4, 5, 6 clubs. Muddle them up and put them on a table face down in four rows of three.

Start a stopwatch.

Turn over two cards at a time. If they match keep them turned over, if they do not, turn them back face down. Your task is to turn over all of the cards as quickly as possible.

If you remember cards that are face down you will be able to do the task faster. Imagine cards with numbers you have already seen as turned over. Try not to turn a card over again until you find its match.

This exercise trains working memory and attention, accelerating the process of perception. Having learned to trust your gut and strengthened your working memory, you will not need to double-check items you have already seen.

21 January 1955

I lead a strange life. By day, I work in the dean's office, and by night, I study at the KGB school.

I thought it would be easier. My head hums and feels like it'll burst after classes. Some exercises (constant, methodical!) make my eyes hurt and water . . . but the results speak for themselves! I was never stupid, but I didn't stand out. I noticed some things (what I wanted to notice and what I was used to noticing) and missed others. I would forget to do things pretty often, could say too much in conversation, walk past someone I knew and not recognize him. Now I notice more and remember things better than before. It helps me understand people better and faster, evaluate and predict situations. I stopped forgetting chores, I barely open my phone book and can do two jobs better than I used to be able to do one. Not to mention how delightful it is when you notice something new and interesting about them . . .

Our most unusual classes are the ones on agent work. They're taught by 'old-timers', who are in their fifties and sixties. I've heard that during the war, a lot of them spent long periods of time behind German lines, but no one knows where exactly. They teach us to strike up conversations with various people, from railroad conductors to company executives. They teach us to code and decode messages, do surveillance, break off a tail, navigate in an unknown city, make invisible ink, take photos and develop microfilm, and a lot of other stuff.

They expect us to notice and memorize a lot of details. For example, they'll take us around the city for an hour, and then ask us what colour the sign over the bakery was, what was posted on the door of the bookstore: 'back after lunch' or 'closed for repairs'. I went back to check afterwards. Turns out it just said 'Closed'. Red paint on grey cardboard.

Unfocused observation

When attention is focused on one item or event, it is likely to miss something important. Therefore, one of the skills necessary for an intelligence officer is unfocused observation. Often, he or she must be able to see the whole picture without concentrating on any specific details. Building on the comparison made earlier between attention and a spotlight, unfocused observation is like diffuse daylight. In order not to miss anything, attention should be focused on the object of observation, and at the same time should be distributed all around.

Exercise

Try watching something without setting any specific goals. For example, you are sitting in a cafe and waiting for someone. Pay attention to the environment without concentrating on anything specific. If you see something interesting, take note of it, but do not narrow your field of view, continue observing all of your surroundings. Do not judge, do not praise, do not criticize - watch indifferently as if everything that is happening is separated from you by thick glass.

★ Train your brain – Matches. Level 1

This exercise has been used to train the visual memory of fighter pilots and intelligence agents for over half a century.

Below, there is a photograph of matches scattered on a table. Memorize their position. After 4 seconds, arrange the matches following the pattern on the page.

There is nothing better for training than old proven methods. If you can remember the location of matches, you will be able to remember a map or drawing at a glance, give a verbal description, or notice that you're being followed.

If you find this exercise interesting, carry a few real matches in your pocket and use them to train during boring lectures and meetings, using a handkerchief to cover up the random arrangement of matches and trying to recreate it on a table. It won't be long before you get results!

2. February 1955

Went to the movies with Z. yesterday, watched The Anna Cross at the Striker. It's funny how differently we saw the movie. Z. cried when Anna was getting married, and the modest fellow (she couldn't remember his full name) made fun of her. But when the heroine of Larion was swept off her feet by a carousel of balls, receptions and speeding carriages, Z. breathed quickly, she couldn't look away, her jaw dropped. She loved the film.

Meanwhile, I, among other things, recognized almost all the real Moscow streets and interiors where the film was shot, memorized all the names from the credits, the costumes and accessories of the characters, the musical theme, the small discrepancies, and then the mass of faces that flashed across the screen in an hour and twenty minutes.

Here it is, the result of all of my training. We were taught to do more than focus on one thing, and to diffuse our attention during observation. This was much harder for me. It seems this time, Z.'s presence heightened my abilities. Suddenly, everything worked, and now I can't get enough of my observational skills.

By the way, we were being watched while we walked along the river after the movie. I guess they're still testing me. We managed to break away by the metro station. It's a bit embarrassing, walking with a girl while under surveillance.

Z. is very attractive, of course, but I doubt it'll work out between us.

★ Train your Brain – Letter pairs, 5×4

This exercise is similar to the one where you were looking for pairs of numbers with playing cards, but instead you use tiles from a word game. Pick any ten letters twice and muddle them face down. Arrange them in five rows of four. Then try and match them. Time yourself and see if you can improve.

Test Yourself

To which Department of the Moscow State University does A. N. Simonov belong?

A) Psychology

B) Philosophy

C) Physics

D) Biology

1
CHIS
(COVERT
HUMAN
INTELLIGENCE
SOURCE)

A CHIS (Covert Human Intelligence Source) agent collects data about people for intelligence services. They find out names, addresses, connections, jobs, positions, lifestyle factors and habits. This data is then collected into documents called 'profiles'.

Most commonly, CHIS agents are recruited from pools of people who have access to personal information about others: public and civil servants, doctors and employment specialists. Valuable information can also be provided by those who see the right kind of people every day, without drawing attention to themselves. They may have the opportunity to view others' desks and . . . their garbage. Pay attention to the concierge at home and the cleaning lady at the office. They may know much more about you than you think.

Many agents begin their career as CHIS. It's a job, a place to train and a test of your abilities.

Memory and imagination

The ability to perceive and remember images is evolutionarily much older and more developed than the ability to understand and remember speech. This is simply because, for our ancestors, a crouching wild animal was more dangerous than a cursing neighbour. It means that any picture, especially a bright, colourful and moving picture, will be perceived faster and better than any text.

How can this be used to improve memory? Try to visualize what you want to remember. For the brain, there is little difference between what is imagined and what is actually seen. An image can be remembered better than text, especially if you imagine it brightly, vividly and in detail.

Here is an example. Your friend explains to you how to get to her or his apartment; they dictate the address: the street name, building and apartment number. Have you memorized it? Then they tell you that they live in a building with a pet store on the ground floor. That's better! Imagine your friend standing behind the counter of the pet store and selling three goldfish to three cats. The apartment number is 33. Yes, it's not real, it is absurd, but it's bright, vivid and unusual, so it's easy to remember.

Exercise

Look at the objects on your desk. Pay attention to all of them. Where are they? How are they arranged? What are the features of each object: colour, texture, wear marks, scratches?

Now, close your eyes. First, imagine the desk, and then start picturing objects one by one. Imagine each of them in detail. If you cannot do it, open your eyes for a while, take a look at the object you had difficulty imagining, then close your eyes and keep picturing.

This exercise can be performed not only with the objects on a table, but with a room, with the view from a window, with people sitting in front of you as you travel.

★ Train your brain – Dice. Level 1

A useful resource for memory training is a selection of different-coloured dice, which can be purchased cheaply, or 'borrowed' from old board games.

This dice exercise is designed to train visual memory and imagination. For this first exercise use two different-coloured dice. Shake the dice out onto a table. Looking at them for only 15 seconds, memorize the colour and number before covering them up or looking away. Without checking, write down both the colour and number.

Taking a mental photograph of the dice on the table and using that to remember should help with this task.

The man who remembered everything

The story of Solomon Shereshevsky, a man with phenomenal abilities, has made its way into all psychology textbooks. Soviet psychologist A. R. Luria was lucky enough to study his memory abilities for three decades, from the 1920s to the 60s.

S. Shereshevsky, or 'S', as Luria called him in his books, could remember any amount of information. He had seemingly unlimited memory. He could recall anything: pictures, concepts, words or meaningless combinations of letters, as if he were reading a book. In addition, it was found that the information he memorized was never erased from his memory. He could effortlessly remember words dictated to him during experiments ten or fifteen years earlier.

Since Shereshevsky's memory could not be measured, Luria tried to describe the way it worked, the mechanisms of remembering and reproducing information.

He found the following:

1. To store information, Shereshevsky encoded it into images. For example, the number 1 was a proud, well-built man, number 6 was a man with a swollen foot, and number 8 was a very stout woman. His ability to encode information into images was innate. Shereshevsky even remembered what he saw and heard in the first months of his life.

2. Shereshevsky had extreme synaesthesia – an intertwining of sensations. People with synaesthesia can clearly distinguish the colour of letters, feel the roughness of sounds and taste shapes. In Shereshevsky's synaesthetic perception, all of his senses were connected, except smell. The images created by the other four of his five senses were very vivid and strong.

3. To remember the order of numbers or items in a long list, Shereshevsky mentally walked down a street in his home town and set images up along the way. Sometimes he 'lost' items from the list. This happened, for example, when the mental image was placed in a dark place, or melted

into the background. At other times, Shereshevsky would imagine his images going on adventures, which evolved into unusual and therefore memorable stories.

The attributes of Shereshevsky's memory that Luria described are used in modern mnemonics.

Exercise

While reading a book, stop and try to conjure up what the author is describing: faces, appearances, objects, interiors, landscapes . . . On the one hand, it will help you to develop your imagination, and on the other to enjoy a good book more deeply and remember its contents better.

9 February 1955

First they taught us to control our attention. A lot. Finally got that. And to focus on one thing and many things at the same time. My head is full of names, numbers and images. Now they're teaching us to work with all of that in our heads — to organize what we need and remove what we don't.

It's like the first grade all over again! Or, rather, like childhood, learning to walk.

I wish spring would come faster. I wonder if this school has vacations.

CHIS

3 March 1955,
Moscow

Case #283
Investigation into missing documents
containing classified information

On 2 March 1955, a report was filed with Police Station
#32 in Moscow regarding the disappearance of Simon
Yakovlevich Bernstein, b. 1897, a member of the
Archives of the Academy of Sciences of USSR. Bernstein
had not been to the Archives since 21 February, but
because of frequent prior absence due to illness,
and the absence of a telephone in his apartment, his
disappearance was only discovered a week later. On 28
February and 1 March, his colleagues attempted to visit
him at home, but no one answered the door either time.

On 2 March, immediately after the disappearance was
reported, Bernstein's room (22 Gorky Street, Apt.15)
was opened in the presence of the district police
officer Senior Lieutenant A. P. Vasiliev. The room was
empty. According to a preliminary examination, none of
Mr Bernstein's personal effects were missing. There were
no signs of a struggle in the apartment.

On the same day, inquiries were made about all people
admitted into hospitals, emergency rooms and morgues in
the Moscow area. There was no one matching Bernstein's
description.

Because Bernstein is the Archives employee responsible
for the storage of classified state documents an
inventory was taken of his section. Some documents
labelled 'Top Secret' were found missing. A list of the
missing documents is attached. Issuance of this list
has not been registered.

Chief Operating Officer
of the Ninth Division
of the Second Main Directorate
Major I. O. Miloslavsky

REFERENCE

to the list of documents

containing classified information missing

from the Archive of the

Academy of Sciences of the USSR.

The missing documents were seized from the archives
of Reich Security Main Office (RSHA) in May 1945. They
belonged to the Amt III of the RSHA (Science), headed
by SS- Gruppenführer Ernst Turowski.

The documents contain the results of theoretical and
experimental studies done by German psychologists and
doctors in the field of suggestive techniques (hypnosis)
for controlling large groups of people. Mostly, these
study results were provided by the German Institute
for Psychological Research and Psychotherapy, known as
the Göring Institute. During the war, the Institute
was headed by Matthias Heinrich Göring, the cousin of
Field Marshal Hermann Göring. Of greatest interest are
the studies of the assistant director of the Institute,
Johann Heinrich Schultz. He is also the author of a
widely known system of autogenic training based on
self-hypnosis. The long-term effectiveness and safety
of autogenic training has been verified on both healthy
subjects and on subjects with personality disorders.

Schultz's books were published in Germany and were
available to any reader. However, many of his works,
as well as the works of other Göring Institute
researchers, are of military value and were classified.
It is undesirable for these documents to fall into the
hands of people and organizations capable of harming
the Soviet Union.

Test Yourself

What movie did Simonov take Z to see?

A) The Searchers

B) The Anna Cross

C) The Maltese Falcon

D) North by Northwest

★ Train your brain – Items on a table. Level 1

It's important for an intelligence officer to remember the location of objects, people, streets and houses – in short, all the little things that are completely uninteresting to most people.

This exercise is used to train and test the memories of young students at intelligence schools. The ability to remember locations of objects is also used by experienced intelligence officers: it helps to determine if anyone was in the room in the absence of its owner.

Take some objects from around your house and place them on a table. Take a photograph. Remember their position. Close your eyes and get a friend or family member to take all the objects off and place them under the table. Try to arrange the items as they were placed earlier. Compare how you did to the photograph.

To perform this exercise, take a 'mental photograph' of the table. Call it up in your mind when you see the empty table. Now arrange the items.

Before arranging the items, you need to imagine the whole table. Some people can do this immediately, but others need to use special methods. One method is to tilt the table in your mind. The items will slide sideways. In what sequence will they fall off the table? To which side? What will crack and break and how? What will the floor look like after all the items fall?

This exercise can be done every day. Look at someone's work desk. Turn around and imagine the position of the items on it. On a bus or train, examine the people sitting across from you. Close your eyes and recreate the picture in your imagination. Look at a bookshelf. Turn around and try to remember the order of the books.

Improving imagination

Imagination might be the most creative function of the brain. With the help of our imagination, we can not only represent what has already been seen, but also create new images. In addition, we can change their size, move them, rotate them, add new elements and remove old ones. It is imagination that people use when coming up with something new: inventors invent, directors make films, writers write books, and artists create paintings.

The creative imagination is used in many mnemonics. As mentioned before, images are easier to remember than text. In order to remember what you have read, you need to see it in your imagination.

Exercise

Spend half an hour blindfolded in your house. Walk around the room. Try, without opening your eyes, to wash your face, dress, or even make breakfast. Turn on some music. Sit in your favourite chair.

Exercise

Imagine a chalk or white board. One that you have seen at school or at home. Imagine the texture of the board, its colour, its frame, the way it hangs on the wall. Maybe it's black, matte and rough, for writing with chalk, or white and smooth, for markers. Now imagine it changing colour to brown. To orange. To blue. Feel each colour. Make the board exactly the colour you want it to be.

When you get to be good at changing the colour of the imaginary board, write any word on it. Look at it closely. How is it written? What colour is the text? What is the texture of the line? Erase the word from the board with an imaginary rag or eraser and write another one. Spend some time with this imaginary board and the words on it.

Come back to this exercise and gradually increase the amount of text. Write short phrases, numbers and lists. Sketch diagrams. Imagine what is written as clearly as possible.

This technique can be very useful for an intelligence officer. Getting stuck on a problem that cannot be solved and returning to it over and over again usually drains mental and physical strength. To break the cycle of unproductive thinking quickly, imagine the problem written on the imaginary board and erase it. Does it pop back up? Erase it! One more time? Erase it! Usually after two or three unsuccessful attempts to return to unproductive thinking, the brain moves on to another topic.

Test yourself

Why was Bernstein's case taken up by
counter-intelligence, not the police?

A) Bernstein was high up in the civil service

B) Bernstein had custody of missing documents
   containing classified information

C) Bernstein was a KGB agent

D) The police were not able to find Bernstein

★ Train your brain – Crossword 4×4

This exercise is designed to train imagination and visual memory.

You can practise this exercise any time you are near a discarded newspaper with a crossword puzzle.

Draw a square consisting of 4x4 squares at each corner of the crossword. Stare at one of the corners, only paying attention to the pattern of dark and light squares. After 4 to 5 seconds, turn over the newspaper and draw the pattern of dark and light squares on the other side of the paper. This exercise is easier if you take a 'mental photograph' of the matrix, and then use it to select the cells. If you can't take a 'mental photograph' right away, group the dark cells into geometric figures.

Once again, it is worth mentioning the importance of spatial reasoning skills. The hypotheses, theories and scenarios an intelligence officer works with have complicated structures. Therefore, the ability to draw them in the form of charts and manipulate them helps keep all the information associated with a complicated assignment in the right frame.

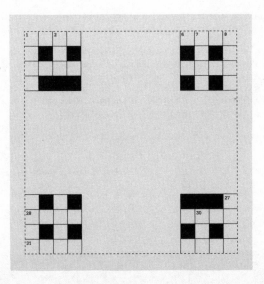

4 March 1955,   <u>CONFIDENTIAL</u>
Moscow

<u>On the investigation</u>
<u>of the missing classified documents</u>
(case #283)

Transfer the investigation to the Chief Operating Officer
of the Second Main Directorate Major I. O. Miloslavsky.

Pursue the following investigative lead: Bernstein has
stolen the classified documents and fled. Consequently,
the investigation must uncover:

1. Bernstein's current whereabouts.

2. The suspect's possible motives.

3. The circumstances of the theft.

It is imperative to determine why the documents were
stolen. If Bernstein had wanted to provide someone with
the contents of the documents, he could have copied them
without stealing or arousing suspicion.

Assign the agent 'Simonides' to determine the value of
the documents and to investigate Bernstein's contacts.

Pursue two lines of investigation. First study the
archivist's personal and business contacts, second
determine who may be interested in obtaining the stolen
documents. The information in the documents is of
military value, so the intelligence service of one of
the capitalist countries may be involved.

Put a warrant out for Bernstein in all USSR republics.

Deputy Chief of
the Second Main Directorate
Colonel V. I. Rukin

March 5, 1955

Didn't get to sleep tonight. Got called into the office for my first assignment in the middle of the night. A man disappeared, 58 years of age. Bemstein. I've seen him around the department a few times. Looks like all the instructors knew Bemstein.

Secret documents that our troops captured in berlin in 1945 have disappeared from the archive. Bemstein was responsible for their safekeeping. I think the two disappearances are related, and this relationship has to be explained. I was tasked with collecting information on Bemstein: who he communicated with, where he spent his time, who he was intimate with and if he had any close friends. I'll report back to my supervisor. According to him, Bemstein could have stolen the documents and gone underground. Or Bemstein could have died or been kidnapped over access to these documents. The second would be better. I'm having trouble suspecting Bemstein. He looked so harmless.

I wonder what was in those documents. I'm curious. I definitely have to get to the bottom of this.

★ Train your brain – Dice. Level 2

Try adding in more dice, with different colours. Only look at them for 10 seconds.

Exercise

Get comfortable, close your eyes and recreate from memory a place you visit often. It can be your favourite coffee shop, an office or a concert hall. Recall the layout of the place. Recall the walls, the floor, the ceiling. How is the furniture arranged? What objects are on the tables and shelves? Imagine yourself sitting at your usual place. What can you see? Try to see the same setting from a different angle: take a different seat, stand on the table or lie down on the floor. What can you see now?

10 March 1955,
Moscow

OPERATIONAL PROFILE
Bernstein, Simon Yakovlevich

Simon Yakovlevich Bernstein was born in Tver in 1897.
Father: Yakov Borisovich Bernstein, b. 1867, tailor.
Died in 1919. Mother: Natalia Nikiforovna Bernstein (née
Eremina), b. 1871. Died in 1925.

Graduated from high school in Tver.

Married E. K. Sosnova in 1918. Divorced in 1921 (E. K.
Sosnova left him for another man). Son, Yakov, born during
marriage in 1920, stayed with father after divorce.

Enrolled in the Philosophy Department of Moscow State
University in 1925. Graduated in 1931. As a student, worked
in a research team led by A. R. Luria and A. N. Leontiev.
Was a test subject in the experiment on changes of
emotional state in response to experimenter's words. After
graduation, remained at MSU as a lecturer. Began writing a
dissertation in the field of child psychology.

Fired from MSU in 1936, after the decree of the Central
Committee of Communist Bolshevik Party 'On Paedological
Perversions in the System of Narkompros (the People's
Commissariat of Education)'. After dismissal, he held
several jobs before gaining employment at the Archives of
the Academy of Sciences of USSR.

Was drafted for military service on the front in 1941
where he served in the infantry. Saw combat. Speaks
German perfectly, has consequently been assigned to work
with captured officers on many occasions. Returned to his
previous job in July 1945.

Bernstein's son Yakov died on the front in 1943. Mr
Bernstein's social circle is confined to professional and
academic colleagues. No close friends.

Signing off — 'Simonides'

11 March 1955

Today, I met with my handler, in secret. I'm going to work on the case of the secret documents directly. We met on Gogol Boulevard, on a bench. During my lunch break. He told me about how we will keep in touch. When I have something to report, I have to come to this square on Tuesday or Friday, to this bench. I can't come to the KGB, yet — I could be being watched. That's not too bad, but there's no reason to draw attention to myself.

It was pretty funny, there was a huge puddle under the bench, and we both sat down on the bench, trying not to get our feet wet and pretending not to know each other.

I told him everything I had found out about Bernstein. It turned out to be a long story. My boss would ask a question if he didn't understand something. Then I went back to work and my boss stayed on the bench.

★ Train your brain – Crossword 5×5

Now draw squares 5x5 on the crossword puzzles. Remember the location of darker cells and recreate them as shapes so it will be easier for you to perform the exercise at higher levels, when the matrix is bigger.

Even if you can do the task without much effort, repeat the exercise several times. Reinforce the skill.

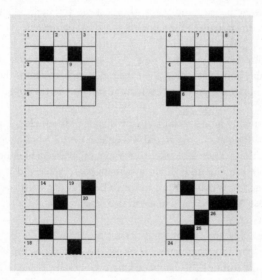

Recalling the forgotten

In some cases, an intelligence officer may have to deal with a member of the public who accidentally witnesses a dramatic event. These types of events can shock someone so much that they only remember one minor detail, forgetting the rest. This can happen, for example, in the case of an armed attack: a witness will only remember the weapon aimed at them and will not recall anything about the attacker's appearance. The goal of an intelligence officer is to help the witness recall what they saw and heard. The most effective method for achieving this is to return the person to the situation they've experienced:

• Meet with your informant in a relaxed atmosphere. Get them comfortable and ask them to close their eyes. Ask questions that will help them to immerse themselves back in the situation in their imagination.

• The informant should recall as many details of the incident as possible. Start with the basics. Where did it happen? Under what circumstances? What did the location look like? How was it lit? Was it cold or hot? Windy? What noises and sounds could a witness hear? What did it smell like? Where was the smell coming from? When did the event occur? What preceded it? What led the witness to this place?

• After recreating the circumstances, start moving towards the event itself in small steps. What happened? How did the witness react to it? What did they feel and think? What happened then? Gradually, step by step, you will come to the information you need. Now, immersed in the situation, they will once again be able to see or hear what needs to be recalled.

To make this method work, it is important to focus the witnesses' memory on the restoration of their feelings and experiences, not of the facts. Remember to use all five senses – sight, hearing, smell, touch, taste.

You may find an instance where you yourself need to recall something important. Your actions in this case would be the same: return to the situation and recall all the feelings and emotions you had.

Recalling a situation through recreation is not necessarily tied only to imagination. If possible, it makes sense to return to the place of the event (preferably at the same time of day) and to try to recollect there.

Exercise

You can use any instance at home in which you've lost a particular item to train recollection. Think back to the last time you were holding the object. What were you doing? How did you use it? Who was at home with you? Who were you talking to? What happened before that? What was your mood? Maybe you were in a hurry, or you were bored? What were you thinking about? How did you use the lost item, and what happened after that? Where did you go with it?

Check the places where you used the lost item and the places where you went after that. If you succeeded in recreating the situation, you will find the missing item much faster than if you had turned the whole house upside down trying to find it.

If someone else has lost an item, perform this exercise with them. If you find the item, be proud of yourself! You helped someone else train their recollection!

★ Train your brain – Pairs, 4×4

Keep on training your working memory. Add in two more of each suit until there are four rows of four cards.

Setting and memory

Memories are often tied to the settings in which they are made. It is much easier to recall the events of school when you are back in the classroom where you spent several years, rather than working in an office. Settings, feelings, sounds and smells can all be associations that help you to draw the past out from memory.

This is more than just an interesting fact. Have you ever been unable to remember the correct answer in an exam, but had it come to mind immediately after you got home? One reason for this may be incorrectly organized memorization. For a student who studied for an exam in pyjamas, sitting in bed with a cup of hot chocolate, the best way to take the exam would be in pyjamas, leaning on pillows and holding a cup. Obviously this isn't possible so it is better to prepare for an exam by sitting at a desk, focused and concentrating.

The setting of learning must match the proposed recall setting. Keep that in mind as you prepare for assignments.

Exercise

To train episodic memory (the memory of events), it is useful to recall the recent past. What happened to you today? How did you wake up? What was your mood? What did you dream about?

Try to remember where you were. What were you doing? Who did you meet with? What were they wearing? What were you talking about? How did you feel when talking to them? Whom did you call and why? What did you eat? What sounds could you hear? Exactly how much money did you spend throughout the day?

Change up the order of recall: on one day, remember the events of the day from morning to evening, on another, reverse the order. Start by recalling one day, then two, three days or all week. Try to remember your day from a week ago. If you perform this exercise every day, you will be able to accurately remember what happened to you in your chosen time slot within a couple of hours. This is a valuable skill in the case of detection.

Test yourself

What does the investigation into the missing classified documents aim to determine? (You may choose more than one answer)

A) Bernstein's current whereabouts

B) The contents of the stolen documents

C) Bernstein's possible motives

D) The circumstances of the theft of the documents

E) The present location of the documents

2
CASE
OFFICER

Agent recruitment

Recruitment of new agents is an extremely serious matter. Recruiting operations are planned well in advance of their implementation. The circumstances and connections of a prospective agent and the potential of access to interesting information are all evaluated. A candidate's personal attributes and suitability to intelligence work are also established.

Depending on the situation, an agent may be recruited for a short period, for the duration of an operation or long term. They may be brought in gradually or offered a large assignment at once. Sometimes agents are recruited under a 'false flag', keeping the real employer hidden. Thus, a young and ambitious employee can be hired by an intelligence service under the cover of a competitor.

The basis for recruitment – an agent's motivation – can also vary. An agent can work for money, for a higher post, or simply for an ideal. Sometimes agents are recruited by blackmail.

Recruitment is sealed with a non-disclosure contract, which has no legal force, but binds the agent morally and can be used as compromising evidence. Sometimes, instead of a non-disclosure contract, the agent can sign a contract for money. After recruitment, an agent is assigned a pseudonym under which they appear in all intelligence documents. This confidentiality is used to protect the source of operative information.

Recruitment is carried out by a case officer – a smart analyst, a sharp psychologist and a perceptive judge of people. They often know how to persuade and inspire people. It is he or she who comes in contact with the future agent, gains their confidence, negotiates working conditions and secures cooperation.

The three principles of mnemonics

Mnemonics are devices that can help develop your memory to enable you to remember facts or large amounts of information.

There are many different mnemonics, but they are all subject to three principles.

1. The use of association

Associativity is a fundamental feature of the psyche. The brain is a perfect machine for building connections between different images and concepts. Memory contains a long and complex chain of associations. If you think of Christmas, at once you imagine a Christmas tree, carols and presents. If a person is thinking about childhood memories, a Christmas tree can bring back thoughts of Santa Claus, gifts and hanging out your stocking. Someone more pragmatic might think of the expense of gift-giving. Someone more religious may think of the Gospel narratives of Jesus's birth.

You already know that the secret of a good memory is not so much remembering as extracting information. It's easier to remember something if it is tied to what you already know. With the help of an association chain, it will be easily recalled when necessary.

Hence the first principle of mnemonics: to remember something, tie it to something that is familiar to you so that you can recall it easily.

2. Coding information with images

You already know how important imagination is for a good memory. Images are easier to remember than words and numbers. Hence the second principle of mnemonics: convert the information you need to remember into pictures.

The first and the second principles of mnemonics are used together. For example, if you need to remember the exact code for an automatic luggage locker being used as a dead letter box: 855411. Perhaps you will need this code a few years from now.

Imagine the numbers in the form of pictures (the principle of coding information through images) and link the images together (the principle of association). The number 8 looks like a plump woman. '5' is a unicycle with one wheel and a seat, '4' is a chair and '1' is a broom. A woman (8) rides on two unicycles (55). One is not enough for her, because she's heavy. In order to keep the unicycles together, she has tied them to a chair (4), on which she sits. But the unicycles are difficult to balance, so, like a tightrope walker, she uses two brooms to stay up (11). She is heading, of course, to the train station, which has luggage storage lockers. Imagine this picture vividly, and the code will not be erased from your memory.

A little advice – it is even better if the concepts are not only visual. Including sound, texture, smell and taste will help you to remember things more clearly. Remember Shereshevsky with his synaesthetic perception. If you imagine a tree, imagine it in detail: it has a large crown with young tender leaves, it smells of fresh sap and it has a warm rough bark on which droplets of sticky, bitter resin glisten.

3. Emotional attitude

People prefer to conserve energy and do not like doing extra work. The brain gives tasks priority depending on the strength of the emotions associated with them. For example, a predator represents a direct threat and causes fear – you have to either fight it or flee it. Extreme thirst would cause concern and forces us to search for water. The smell of rotten food causes disgust, which protects from possible poisoning. Events associated with strong emotions make us learn – avoiding predators' trails, remembering the way to a water source and avoiding spoiled food.

Emotions activate memory. If you ask the average person to recall events that occurred a few years ago, they will most likely remember milestones in their life: the birth of children, meeting or parting with a life-partner, moving, changing jobs or exciting travel. All of these events caused strong emotions when they occurred, and that's why they are so memorable. The rest, as a rule, is erased from memory as something ordinary, not worthy of interest. In other words, you only remember what you need to remember, what you really care about.

The third principle of mnemonics is: establish an emotional attitude towards the memorized information. Do you remember the locker code from the previous principle? Why do you think that is? Partly because you were surprised or confused by the comically absurd image of a woman riding unicycles tied to a chair, trying to keep her balance with two brooms. You will study mnemonic techniques. Do not be put off by their absurdity – it is good because it causes emotional responses, and thus allows you to remember well and recall quickly.

Notes

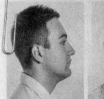

AGENT REP[

- - - - - - - - - - - - - - -

Re: Case #283
14 March 1955
Source: 'Simonides'
Received by: Major I. O. Miloslavsky

- -

On Bernstein's connections (transcribed from audiotape)

His job as archivist allowed Bernstein to communicate with
prominent Moscow State University scientists. Many, for example
A. N. Leontiev, A. R. Luria and B. M. Teplov, consulted him
about materials for monographs, articles and dissertations.

At the same time, his communication was limited to professional
relationships. He did not have a family: his wife left him
before the war and his son was killed at the Leningrad front.
All his contacts are somehow connected to psychology. Bernstein
barely communicated with his neighbours. He had no close
friends. The only exception is V .M. Kovalev.

Vasily Mikhailovich Kovalev was born in Leningrad in 1930. He
is a psychologist and graduated from MSU. He is a graduate
student currently writing a dissertation on the psychology of
large groups.

Kovalev has a close relationship with Bernstein. Bernstein
became a sort of mentor to him and helped him in various
difficult situations. This is not only in relation to research.
Bernstein helped Kovalev obtain a dormitory room when he
entered graduate school. They met regularly. The meetings
lasted several hours. Over tea, Bernstein and Kovalev discussed
various topics.

Kovalev resembles Bernstein's son who was killed at the front.
This may explain Bernstein's paternal attitude towards Kovalev.

- -

Note: tape is demagnetized
Assignment: explore relationships between Kovalev and Bernstein
Activities: put Kovalev under surveillance (subject 'Poet')

#134

Associations

The associations that we use for memorization can be very different.

1. Similarity in appearance, function, spelling or sound. The bases for similarity can be:

–   The number 8 is similar to a plump woman, to glasses seen from above, or to the infinity sign;

–   A plane flies, which makes it similar to a bird, a parachute and a kite;

–   The Spanish word la bandera (meaning flag) contains the familiar word band. You will notice that flags in the Middle Ages consisted of a band or strip of fabric.

2. Contrast: light and dark, salty and sweet, male and female.

3. Cause and effect: clouds bring rain, fire creates heat and banana peel can cause someone to slip.

4. Integration in time and space:the Kremlin is in Moscow, the Bronze Horseman is in Saint Petersburg, Leonardo da Vinci lived in the Renaissance.

History confirms the importance of association for remembering. Many ancient texts – epics, legends, sagas, scientific treatises and collections of medical prescriptions – were created in verse form. Metre, rhyme, harmony and repetition – these associations between words helped our ancestors memorize the great texts.

There is a rule in memory improvement: the more you know, the easier it is for you to remember. Someone with a vast system of knowledge can more easily connect new data to information they already have.

Exercise

The ability to quickly pick associations and tie a variety of things together is an integral part of any mnemonic. You can develop this skill by practising regularly. Try to link two different items that you can see. How can you connect a door knob and a paper clip? Is their curved shape similar? Or can you melt a pack of paper clips to cast a knob? Or simply attach a paper clip to the knob?

★ Train your brain – Word pairs. Level 1

Learning to make associations between words is important for all the mnemonics described in this book. Pay attention to this exercise.

Below are a few pairs of words. You need to remember them.

Make associations linking the words in each pair. Pick images to remember these associations. Close the book for 60 seconds.

Once the time for memorization is up, say the words and their pairs out loud. How many did you remember?

Watermelon/bat

Helicopter/dress

Tree/telephone

Flowers/puddle

Camera/coins

Pillow/carrots

Truck/teddy bear

Magnet/paintbrush

Keys/fork

Cinder block/chair

<u>INTERROGATION RESULTS</u>

15 March 1955,
Moscow

Pursuant to further surveillance of Kovalev we do not
consider interrogating him at KGB headquarters prudent.
In order to obtain information about Bernstein's
disappearance, an interrogation was conducted in
Kovalev's room at the Moscow State University dormitory.
Kovalev was not informed of the disappearance of the RSHA
documents.

During the interview, Kovalev behaved nervously. He
answered questions reluctantly and tersely. Denied
friendship with Bernstein, saying that they communicated
only about the dissertation and only in the course of
brief consultations. Claims that he last saw Bernstein a
long time ago, maybe a few weeks, does not remember when
exactly.

A search of Kovalev's room was not made, but its
appearance is notably different from other students'
rooms. Specifically, Kovalev has an expensive gramophone
and many records. When questioned as to the origin of
these things, Kovalev said that he bought them in a
thrift shop using money given to him by his parents for
graduation.

Chief Operating Officer
of the Second Main Directorate
Major I. O. Miloslavsky

★ Train your brain – Word pairs. Level 2

Keep on developing skills in building associations. This list of word pairs is longer and trickier – have a go at memorizing them all! If you're finding it too hard, try splitting the list in half.

Commander/zebra

Fish tank/cookery book

Scissors/lime

Tennis racquet/sunscreen

Sponge/hammer

Apple/wishbone

Dinosaur/peanut butter

Credit card/chocolate

Rolling pin/screwdriver

Toothpick/teapot

Salt shaker/sword

CD/bottle of soda

Steak knife/bow tie

Rubber band/pine cone

Perfume/martini glass

Lists of words

The ability to memorize lists of words is a significant milestone in improving memory. Firstly, it will allow you to show off! You can impress your friends by repeating forty dictated words from the first to the last. Secondly, it will allow you to memorize a list of daily chores, the minutes of a meeting or a plan of your speech.

An intelligence officer who can memorize lists of words can also remember passwords, legends, scripts and contact information. Words are associated with facts, and links can be found between seemingly independent events.

There are two basic techniques for memorizing a list of words: the story method and the method of loci (places). You will learn both techniques and be able to use them for different situations. However, you may prefer to stick to one method, while minimally trying the other. Decide for yourself.

The story method

This method consists of developing a story that ties together the words you need to remember by visualizing it and saturating it with emotions. The story can be absurd, and the more absurd it is, the stronger the list will stick in your memory. Here is another secret: put yourself into the story to give it significance and make it more memorable.

For example, here is a list of words:

```
oil;

table;

taxi driver;

coffee;

code;

tree;

balcony.
```

Here is a story you might construct.

You are in a dark tavern in a port town. The sea rumbles outside, you can hear ship horns and the shouts of dockside workers. There is a barrel of oil near the window, it is made of rusted iron and emits the sharp odour of heating oil. The barrel is covered with a round wooden shield. At it, as if at a table, sits a taxi driver wearing a velvet jacket and drinking black coffee. He will be driving, so rum, the standard drink of the tavern, is not available for him. The bitter smell of coffee is mixed with the smell of heating oil. The taxi driver has to pick up a passenger at the port, but he cannot, because the passenger's name is encrypted, and the driver does not know the code. The taxi driver is looking sullenly at the sheet of yellowed paper with gibberish printed on it. But then you receive a text message saying that the cipher key is in the tree outside the tavern. Surprised, you show the message to the taxi driver and run outside with him. The taxi driver is trying to climb the tree, but he keeps failing, because the trunk is smooth and slippery. So he goes up to the second floor of the tavern, steps out onto the balcony, and from there climbs a tree and finds an envelope with the code.

Did you visualize the story? Now repeat the list of words. Try to do it in reverse order. Did it work?

Note that we used all three principles of mnemonics. The story itself is a series of associations. Words are encoded with vivid images: the rusty stinking barrel, soft velvet, bitter black coffee, yellowed paper, etc. The participants of this story are experiencing emotions: the taxi driver is sullen, you're surprised at the unexpected message, and the story ends with a 'happy ending'.

Exercise

Remember the geography of the place where you live. If there is a subway in the city, remember the metro map. Each branch is a list of stations. Make sure you can repeat the names of the stations in any order. Memorize all of the branches. Over time, you will be able to navigate the metro just from memory. Similarly, you can remember the sequence of streets, bus stops, etc. It can be useful when you want to break away from a surveillance or use a cover story.

★ Train your brain – Word list. Story method. Level 1

You will be shown a list of words. Remember it and reproduce it in its original order.

Remember this list using the story method. Being able to make associations, a skill acquired while memorizing pairs of words, will help you in this exercise. Master the story method using short lists before moving on.

pirate ship

dog

safety goggles

wedding ring

letter opener

acorn

 <u>AGENT REPORT</u>

- -
Re: Case #283
21 March 1955
Source: 'Simonides'
Received by: Major I. O. Miloslavsky
- -

<u>On the value of the missing documents</u>

Today I consulted with Professor Luria about the research
value of the missing classified documents. I showed the
professor a list of the documents and their themes/
sources, under the cover that this is a list of materials
collected for a dissertation.

A. R. Luria has evaluated these documents as being of
interest, though requiring considerable refinement before
they can be applied practically. However, he evaluated
the prospects of such refinement within the Soviet Union
as low: the topic is considered unscientific by the
Soviet school of psychology, and the use of suggestive
methods on large groups unacceptable for ethical reasons.
Nonetheless, according to Luria, such implementation is
possible in capitalist countries, especially for military
purposes.

#156

22 March 1955

Met with Luria yesterday. Tried to get his opinion on
the missing documents. This meeting definitely shows
how far my new work can take me. Though he
didn't tell me anything particularly important, it's always
pleasant to spend nearly an hour in conversation with
a very intelligent person. He's lectured us before, but
that's completely different from a personal conversation.
Now, looking back, I realize I was truly impressed,
which is a rare feeling for me. He's tall, with a broad
forehead. With a spark of grey in his black hair. A
thoughtful, sharp gaze. Clear, precise speech. This
calm awareness of his own importance. His work with
the wounded during the war, his research on the brain
. . . all of this deserves my respect.

Now that my fire has cooled a bit, I wonder, (1) Did
he use any sort of suggestive techniques in conversation
with me? (2.) Maybe he's working for the office, too?

★ Train your brain – Word list. Story method. Level 2

Keep on training with the story method to memorize lists. This one is longer and you should time how long it takes you repeat the information back after memorizing.

Construct vivid emotional stories, imagine them. Use images, sounds, smells, sensations from touching the item. Include yourself in the story.

```
postage stamp

bottle of oil

marble

octopus

spool of wire

chalk

book

rubber gloves

toy soldier

jigsaw
```

Images of abstract concepts

It is usually easy to picture images of things and objects. When you say 'cup', you imagine your favourite cup, which has shape, colour and weight. 'Road' will evoke a familiar section of road in your imagination. But what do you do with abstract concepts that have no tangible expression, such as 'salary', 'happiness' or 'suggestion'?

There are two ways of re-coding such concepts into images. The first is based on what the word sounds like. You pick a word or words that sound similar to the one that you want to remember. Then you encode this similar word or words into the image. For example, you can use 'celery' for 'salary', 'happy nest' for 'happiness.'

The second method uses symbolic imagination: you intuitively pick a specific image or symbol to express the abstract concept. This word can be generally accepted or unique to you. So for liberty, you might picture the Liberty Bell; for happiness, a smiley face.

If you want to use symbols, 'agreement' can be imagined as a firm handshake or as the Egyptian obelisk in the Place de la Concorde in Paris. 'Duty' may be represented as an official document with a seal.

Association and symbols are very individual. For a student of the Middle Ages, the word 'suggestion' is associated with the name of Abbot Suger, who lived in the eleventh to twelfth century and devoted himself to the reorganization and reform of Saint-Denis near Paris. The broader a person's scope of knowledge, the easier it is to pick up new associations and remember new information.

Exercise

Take a glossary of terms from a field you are unfamiliar with: engineering, philosophy or psychology. Open it at random and try to create images for the words you find, using phonetic and symbolic associations.

24 March 1955,
Moscow

<u>On the investigation of
the missing classified documents</u>
(file with case #283)

Based on agent information, the current lead is
that the documents were stolen by foreign agencies
or persons interested in the resurgence of Nazi
ideology.

Activities: evaluate the activity of intelligence
services in capitalist countries and pro-Nazi
organizations in the scientific community. Determine
what, if any, connections exist between known foreign
agent networks and the disappearance of classified
RSHA documents.

> Chief Operating Officer
> of the Second Main Directorate
> Major I. O. Miloslavsky

★ Train your brain – Word pairs. Level 3

Open a book at any page and remember the first word on each line. If you encounter a preposition or part of a word carried over from the previous page, take the next word. Remember the words, using the word pair method, close the book, marking your page. Repeat the list and check yourself. You can test yourself by doing the same with newspaper articles.

Test yourself

Why did S. Y. Bernstein, who avoided close relationships, get to be close friends with graduate student V. M. Kovalev?

A) Kovalev was a friend of Bernstein's dead son

B) Kovalev reminded Bernstein of his son

C) Kovalev helped Bernstein to obtain a dormitory room

D) Bernstein was interested in the psychology of large groups, and Kovalev was an expert in it

26 March 1955,
Moscow

REFERENCE

From 1933 to 1945, the Nazis conducted experiments on
prisoners of concentration camps, which usually led
either to their death or irreversible damage to their
health.

These experiments have already been carried out
and it is impossible to repair their consequences.
However, it is unspoken that some of the results
obtained from these experiments are used now, for
example in saving people who have suffered from
disasters.

Many of the 'killer doctors' who performed
experiments on concentration camp inmates escaped
retribution. The most famous of them, Josef Mengele,
hid in Bavaria for a few years after the war and,
according to reports, fled to Argentina afterwards.

At the Nuremberg trials in 1946—47, twenty-three
people were accused of medical experiments on
concentration camp inmates. Seven of them were
sentenced to death, five were imprisoned for life,
four were sentenced to various prison terms and seven
were acquitted. Most of those who were imprisoned
have since been released early and now work in
military and medical institutions in Germany and the
USA.

Colonel K. N. Stolin
of the Second Main Directorate

Memorizing phrases

The ability to memorize lists of words quickly and invent visual stories opens up the possibility of remembering greater quantities of information, specifically phrases and pieces of text.

For example, you are being briefed for a new job and are told to memorize the password: 'Bill Brown said that the cranes will be delivered next week.' One way to remember this story is to picture Bill Clinton (Bill) in a very dirty uniform, making it seem brown (Brown), standing at a construction site. He is very gloomy and sad (said). Bill is looking up at two big yellow cranes (cranes). One of them has a pegboard on its door with a bunch of different delivery menus attached (delivery) and a calendar on with the next week blocked off in highlighter (next week).

Try to forget this phrase now.

Exercise

```
Make up visual stories for proverbs, sayings and phrases you
know.
```

CONFIDENTIAL

<u>AGENT REPORT</u>

- -
Re: Case #283
28 March 1955
Source: 'Simonides'
Received by: Major I. O. Miloslavsky
- -

<u>On Kovalev's personality and lifestyle</u>

At present, gathering information on Mr Kovalev —
his lifestyle, interests and research projects.

Kovalev has been a graduate student for two years.
He is not very successful but meets expectations.

Not independent. Dependent on other people's
judgements and opinions.

Parents, Mikhaill Ilyich Kovalev and Elena Viktorovna
Kovaleva, engineers. Live in Leningrad. Rented room
for son while he was studying at MSU. However,
once son entered graduate school, insisted that he
should move to the dormitory and stopped sending him
money. Father believes that his son should achieve
everything for himself.

At the same time, Mr Kovalev's cash expenses are
rather high. In particular, he is interested in
popular music, buys a lot of records, including those
of foreign origin.

For the past half year, Kovalev has developed an
interest in art, especially in paintings of the
European Late Middle Ages. Goes to museums and
exhibitions regularly. Buys expensive catalogues of
reproductions.

#230

★ Train your brain – Items on a table. Level 2

Gather more objects from around your house, perhaps focusing on ones you are less familiar with. Put them out on the table or get someone to do it for you. Once again, mentally take a photograph of the table, then cover the items over with a tablecloth and imagine this picture when mentally placing the items back on the table.

Notes

TOP SECRET

AGENT REPORT

- -
Re: Case #283
9 April 1955
Source: 'Simonides'
Received by: Major I. O. Miloslavsky
- -

On agent recruitment

In accordance with received authorization, the following
MSU students and staff were recruited:

Arkhipov Y. I., b. 1935, 3rd year student

Mihin V. R., b. 1929, postgraduate student

Rychko L. S., b. 1920, senior lecturer

V. M. Kravchuk refused to cooperate with the KGB

Contact with new agents was delegated to an agent,
Lieutenant Prikhotko E. Y.

#168

10 April 1955

I recruited my first informants today. All that training is paying off. Managed to win their trust. Managed to get people interested in working with us.

Kravchuk didn't go along with it, though. But I hope I at least managed to convince him not to talk about our conversation.

Memorizing foreign language vocabulary

Foreign language education is routine for intelligence training. Intelligence officers are chosen for their mental abilities, and to teach them to speak any language fluently and without an accent is a matter of technique.

At the initial stage of studying a language, a student must memorize pairs of words, one of which is known (in the native language), and the other of which is not (in the foreign language). The following algorithm is used.

1. The known word in the native language is encoded with an image. You know this technique from the story method.

2. The second (unknown) word is easier to code by phonetic similarity: pick one or more words in the native language so that they are phonetically similar to the foreign word.

3. Tie the image of the word in the native language to the images of words which resemble the foreign word in one story.

For example, you need to remember the French word grognon (which means 'grumpy'). It is consonant with the word 'groan', so to memorize the pair 'grognon–grumpy' you can imagine a grumpy man groaning in irritation.

With practice, you will learn to create these stories quickly and remember at least fifty to seventy foreign words in one session.

Exercise

Buy a small dictionary with 500-1000 of the most common words in a language that you've always wanted to learn. Using the method described above, you will be able to remember them pretty quickly, and it will be a good way to start realizing your dream.

16 April 1955

I'm collecting information on Kovalev. I think Arkhipov,
Rychko and Mihin, whom I've recruited, are doing the
same thing, but I haven't spoken to them since. They're
avoiding running into me, and Rychko actually turns away
and pretends to be reading the newspaper when
I walk by him.

Kovalev is a curious character. He's good at school,
doesn't over exert himself. None of his classmates have
ever seen him poring over books, but he's got Bs and
As in all of his exams. Got into grad school on a
recommendation. Doesn't add particular effort to his
natural skills — he's at the cafe a lot, with records or
books of art prints.

Bemstein was helping Kovalev, and Kovalev has
something to do with the case of the missing documents.
And he knows something about Bemstein, too, but he
refuses to say anything.

It turns out the documents that disappeared fro the
archive are actually really important. They contain protocols
and experimental results on mind control. It's not quite
control, to be honest. The fascists sprayed this gas
into concentration camp barracks and this gets rid of a
person's free will, so they turn into an obedient animal.
There were monographs on mass hypnosis in there, too,
something about autogenic training and a lot of other
stuff. None of it, except the book on autogenic training,
has ever been published and exists in only the one copy.

It looks like the Germans were going to use these ideas for military purposes, but didn't have time to finalize it. I can't imagine what would happen if these documents fall into the hands of today's war hawks.

Test yourself

What is the case number of the investigation of the missing classified documents?

A) 286

B) 283

C) 1955

D) 9

E) 236

★ Train your brain – Word dictation. Story method. Level 1

It is now time to increase the pace. As you flick through a book, look at the word in the bottom line of each right-hand page and find the first noun. Allow yourself only five seconds on each word before turning to the next one. At first, it may be difficult for you to get into the pace of changing words. However, gradually you will be able to invent stories faster, and the use of mnemonics will become unconscious, like reading or writing.

18 April 1955

Call Vasily Mikhailovich Kovalev for questioning about
the disappearance of Bernstein. Do not mention the
loss of documents from the Archives of the Academy of
Sciences of USSR during the interrogation.

> Chief Operating Officer
> of the Second Main Directorate
> Major I. O. Miloslavsky

FOR OFFICAL USE ONLY

19 April 1955,
Moscow

(File with Case #283)

REFERENCE

The hypnotic trance is a special psychological state that combines both sleep and awareness. It is accompanied by increased suggestibility: people may readily take for granted under hypnosis what they otherwise would never believe.

Modern understanding of hypnosis is based on the works of French psychiatrists Jean Charcot and Hippolyte Bernheim (19th century). Russian scientist V. M. Behterev also studied hypnosis. However, despite long-standing scientific interest in this phenomenon, little is known about the mechanisms of hypnosis.

The use of hypnosis during performances for large audiences shows that it works on some people but not others. It is likely that different people are susceptible to hypnotism to different levels. Famous hypnotist Wolf Messing selects easily suggestible people for his performances.

During Messing's performances, hypnotized people can lie across two chairs supported only by their head and feet. They can bear weights of several tens of kilograms placed on their stomachs. People do not feel pain, they reveal more information about themselves than they normally would and perform the strangest tasks for the hypnotist.

Many hypnotists claim that they are able to hypnotize anyone at any time, but it is not true. At the level to which hypnotism has developed today, the person being hypnotized has to help the hypnotist in inducing a trance. Scientists, including military scientists, are working on new methods of hypnosis that would allow an influence on any person against their will, but these methods have not yet been developed.

Colonel K. N. Stolin
of the Second Main Directorate

Motivation to remember

A person's motives and needs have a great impact on memory. For example, you will probably find trying to remember all the stops on your railway line difficult. This is because you don't need this information, unless, of course, you are a conductor who gives out information about these destinations every day. In that case, you would be likely to remember them without putting any intentional effort into memorizing them.

It's easier to remember information you need day-to-day. The brain prefers to conserve its energy by separating what is important from the rest of the information it receives. This leads to the following practical recommendation: before you try to memorize anything, define for yourself why you want to remember it and what you will get from knowing it. Similarly, if you want someone to remember something you ask him/her, create a trigger for him/her to remember. Get him/her interested. Specify when and under what conditions they should recall the request. For example, if you want your neighbour to drop a letter in a postbox, tell him: 'Bob, when you pass by the pillar box remember my request, drop the letter in. I would really appreciate it.' The words 'when you . . .' will help a person to remember about the request at the right time. Your appreciation will be an additional emotional stimulus for Bob.

Needs and motivations often play a cruel joke with memory. Sigmund Freud, the founder of psychoanalysis, describes its mechanisms. The human desire for emotional comfort often makes us forget information that may be unpleasant. Freud called this phenomenon 'repression'.

If you always forget about meetings with a specific person, although this rarely happens for meetings with other people, look at the situation more closely. Perhaps communicating with that person causes emotional discomfort. It is hard to imagine that someone would forget to call a generous friend to ask for money. But a debtor often forgets to call a creditor to ask for an extension.

★ Train your brain – Matches. Level 2

It's time to complicate the match exercise. Increase the number of matches, and get someone else to throw them down on the table for you.

Change the exercise up a bit by using a mixture of matches and pencils. Try and recreate the pattern on paper. Here is one to get you started.

SURVEILLANCE RESULTS FOR THE 'POET'

21 April 1955,
Moscow

The subject was in his MSU dorm room at Stromynka Street on 21
April 1955 until 12:20. At 12:20 he went out and took the #14
bus towards the Kievskaya metro station. At 12:50 he was walking
beside the train in the direction of the Krasnopresnenskaya
station. Two agents of the Seventh Division followed him using
the fork technique. Just before the train's departure, he held
open the closing doors and jumped into the train. An attempt to
find him following in the next train failed.

Kovalev was found only at 15:00, in the Moscow State University
building. At 15:50 he took a tram headed to Sokolniki Park.
Lieutenant Chinarev led surveillance. At 16:40, the target sat at
a table in a park cafe and ordered two ice creams. He attempted
to make the acquaintance of a young woman, inviting her to his
table, but was rejected.

At 18:35 the target left the park and headed to the dorm. I took
over surveillance, using the leading method.

At 19:05 the object entered the dorm and went to the third floor,
where his room is located. The agent following him went to the
next floor up and then went down to the first floor and remained in
the guard room. 15 minutes later, at 19:20, student K. N. Bykov
ran to the security guard and asked him to call a doctor, because
one of the third-floor residents had become ill.

I went up to the third floor and found the 'Poet' lying in the
hallway. He displayed no signs of life or palpable pulse. 10
minutes later, at 19:30, an emergency doctor came and confirmed
the death, presumably from acute heart failure.

I immediately made a cursory examination of the 'Poet's' room.
Nothing suspicious was found.

At 20:00 Lieutenant Chinarev and I came back to the cafe and
attempted to obtain the dishes the target had used, but the
plates and cups had already been washed. The same ice cream had
been eaten by other visitors of the cafe, but their health was
normal.

Chief Operating Officer
of the Seventh Division
Captain V. Nikiforov

CONFIDENTIAL

#36g

2. April 1955

They gathered us up last night and told us that
Kovalev is dead. He was probably murdered. We had
wanted to use him to get on the trail of Bernstein or
the archive documents. Alas — we'll have to start over.

Forgetting curve

At the end of the nineteenth century, German psychologist Hermann Ebbinghaus constructed the forgetting curve, showing how people tend to forget information they had learned. Ebbinghaus asked subjects to remember meaningless three-letter syllables. Using rote learning, without imagination, an hour later we can recall only 44% of the learned information, and in a week – less than 25%. Fortunately, with conscious memorization, information is forgotten more slowly.

The majority of information is forgotten within the first hours after learning. What can be done? Further experiments showed that repetition reduces the rate of forgetting. The more you repeat the information, the better you will remember it.

Experiments determining the rate of forgetting have formed practical conclusions. The first is that attempting to memorize anything in one sitting is not effective. It's better to memorize information in stages, leaving time for repetition.

If you have one day for memorization, the optimal rate of repetition is as follows:

- the first time, 15 to 20 minutes after learning;

- the second time, after 6 to 8 hours;

- the third time after 24 hours.

It's better to repeat information actively: rather than listening or reading a second time, try to draw or write it from memory and check against the source if necessary.

If you have more time for memorization, repeat the information as follows:

- the first time the day of first learning;

- the second on the fourth day afterwards;

- the third on the seventh day afterwards.

If there is a lot of information, it is better to repeat it with different amounts of detail: the first time in full, the second time just the key points, and the third time all the information, but in a different group or in a different order. The deeper the level of processing, the easier the information is to recall.

Threefold repetition is the required minimum. When an intelligence officer learns his/her cover story, s/he repeats it a hundred times, and then returns to it regularly, refreshing his/her memory. After all, it's a matter of life or death.

★ Train your brain – Crossword 6×6

This time draw squares 6 by 6 around the corners of the crossword puzzle. Try and memorize them as quickly as you can.

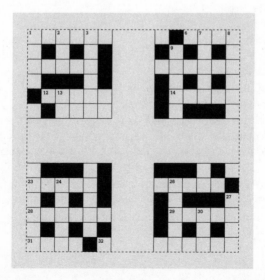

Serial position effect

This memory effect is very important for intelligence officers. To test it, let's conduct a little experiment. Read the following words quickly and without preparation:

fireworks

orange

car

clock

sofa

painting

algebra

doctor

magazine

staff

skyscraper

meteorite

Close the book and try to recall the words. Now.

Check yourself. The words 'fireworks' and 'meteorite' are the ones you were most likely to remember. The words from the middle of the list will be more difficult to recall correctly. So, the beginning and the end are easier to remember.

Serial position effects don't only work with lists. When you're trying to recall the events of the day, morning and evening are often recalled more clearly. When memorizing a story, the hardest part is its chronological middle.

As already mentioned, the serial position effect is widely used in the intelligence service. You can use it to disguise your interest in a topic. You should not talk about things that really interest you at the beginning and at the end of a conversation. Start with an abstract theme. In the middle of the conversation ask or tell what you need. At the end of the conversation talk about something else.

The serial position effect does not always work. If you touch on topics that are extremely painful for a person, they will remember it anyway, even if you pick it up in the middle of a conversation. The art of the intelligence officer involves knowing the sore spots and avoiding them.

You can ask the question differently. For example, you can create the impression of being a small-minded and tactless person who brings up an uncomfortable topic because of his/her ignorance or thoughtlessness. In this case, your interlocutor will remember your clumsy faux pas and push the question you asked into the background.

★ Train your brain – Schulte Tables, 5×5

Here is another Schulte Table for you to try.

Remember, focus on the middle cell of the table. Look for the numbers with your peripheral vision. Try to see more than just the number that you need at the moment.

Keep coming back to this exercise. It trains the mind, teaches you to observe and plan actions in advance.

16	24	6	20	3
25	8	5	13	21
12	10	17	4	18
2	7	15	22	9
14	23	16	1	11

23 April 1955,
Moscow

<u>On the investigation</u>
<u>of the missing classified documents</u>
(file with case #283)

Based on current circumstances, it is worthwhile to develop
two main versions of the events associated with the missing
classified documents.

Version One: Bernstein has escaped with the documents from
the Archives, Kovalev is not involved in the case, and his
death is a consequence due only to the state of his health.

Version Two: Bernstein stole the documents, Kovalev somehow
found out about it and Bernstein killed him with a slow-
acting poison. Autopsy shows that Kovalev died of a heart
attack, however his medical examination at the university
hospital two months prior showed no cardiac abnormalities.

Death from a heart attack is unlikely, so the possibility
of murder cannot be excluded. Moreover, the autopsy shows
that between 13:00 and 14:00 Kovalev had lunch and drank
approximately 100 to 200 ml of red wine, so he could have
been poisoned then.

To test both versions, it is necessary to retrieve
information about Kovalev's interests, contacts and
circumstances in the last weeks of his life.

Simultaneously, actively organize a set-up. Use the help of
an agent under the cover of a specialist who has access to
developments in the field of mass suggestive techniques.

Because there may be a foreign intelligence agent in
Moscow, the Second Main Directorate has instructed an
acceleration of this investigation, of the search for the
missing documents and detainment of the criminal.

Deputy Chief
of the Second Main Directorate
Colonel V. I. Rukin

Interference

The essence of interference is that similar memories get mixed up. Two similar memories influence each other, and the more alike they are, the harder it is to remember them reliably. It is not only new information that makes it difficult to recall old information, but, on the contrary, often old information interferes with the reproduction of new memories.

For example, you use a bank card for a couple of years and remember its PIN perfectly. The card expires and the bank issues you a new one. Initially, each time you are at the ATM, the old PIN will automatically pop up in your memory, so that it will take a conscious effort to recall the new one. But after a while this habit will change: the new PIN will be recalled automatically and the old one will take effort. Similar memories associated with the same situation interfere with each other.

To reduce the impact of interference, you can separate the memorization of similar information in time. For example, when preparing for an exam, try to memorize points which are as different from each other as possible together. This rule holds true in many cases: the change of activity saves energy. If on a given day, you need to edit a document, write a review and draw a diagram, then it is better to separate the text editing and review from each other with drawing the diagram.

Conversely, if you want someone to forget something, ply them with plenty of information on a related topic. Ask for their opinion, discuss the topic in detail, and involve them closely. As a result, there will be a lot of information, which will lead to confusion, and thanks to the interference, they will not be able to remember what you want them to forget as clearly as they would have otherwise. At the very least, they will be confused and lose confidence.

When someone tries to remember something in a conversation and you want to prevent this, try to prompt him/her. Incorrect, but similar, suggestions will prevent recollection, creating interference. This technique is used by attorneys, confusing witnesses during court proceedings.

In everyday life, you can see this happening when your friends or family are trying to help you to remember something, which usually only makes it harder.

★ Train your brain – Dice. Level 3

Add in more coloured dice and give yourself only 5 seconds to remember the numbers and colours.

Notes

Manners and habits

Interference is not just about memorizing information. It also applies to skills. For example, people from countries with right-hand traffic are confused in countries with left-hand traffic. The 'right-hand' skill is not only useless, but also interferes with the new situation. We have to make an effort to overcome it.

In a tense situation, when conscious control is weakened, old habits can re-emerge. There are cases in the history of intelligence services when involuntary actions betrayed undercover agents.

The KGB once distributed a memo with a list of features that can be used to identify foreign agents. It mentions, for example, putting ice into alcoholic beverages, offering to pay for small favours, eating dinner without bread, etc. This behaviour is perfectly normal for the residents of Western Europe and the USA, but it is not typical for Soviets.

Do you want the person to show their old habits? Touch on a sensitive topic or confuse them by making them respond quickly to words and actions. It is likely that they will give themselves away while distracted. Fatigue or alcoholic intoxication also weaken conscious control and can serve as the means to identify the hidden habits of a person.

25 April 1955

The last few days have been loaded with work
and studying like never before. Any hope for a quick
investigation died with Kovalev. What's left is a lot of
very meticulous work to do every day. If not for training,
which continues as intensely as usual, I would say the
work is boring. On my way home yesterday, I finally
saw all of its beauty and wonder. Everything they ever
taught us in school and at university fell into place.
All of a sudden, people's thoughts and feelings, their
words and actions, their relationships to each other,
became a lot clearer. And now I have the ability to
affect all of this.

I looked at the passengers in the metro and saw
how they had spent the day (or even the week!).
The expressions on their faces, their postures, their
clothing, shoes, even the bag they're holding can tell
me so much. I was in such a good mood that when
I left the metro, I kissed two women I didn't know.
They thought I was either drunk or crazy. When I
asked them if they knew where I could buy flowers
at this hour, and if they knew where maternity ward
18 was, they thawed a bit and giggled, saying they
couldn't help. I disappeared into the darkness, the girls
remained, discussing the 'young father', forgetting the
insolent kisser.

People remember the last thing they hear in a
conversation — just as we were taught.

Partial reproduction and forgetting

You may have noticed this effect yourself when you have not had time to study all the material for an exam. The question that you didn't study for because you thought the topic is the one that's the most difficult to answer during an exam.

For someone who remembers a lot of information about an event, it's more difficult to recall a specific detail if they were asked about another detail before. It will be more difficult for a witness to describe the colour of an offender's jacket if they were first asked about the shape of the attacker's glasses. This pattern is often used to confuse a witness in court, especially if they only had a glimpse of the offender. By asking questions about minor details and interrupting at the right time, a manipulative lawyer dents a witness's confidence and catches them on discrepancies in their testimony.

If you want your informant to forget about a question that you asked, at the next meeting with them, go over all the other questions again. The informant will put the original question out of their mind, or at least let it recede in their memory. Consider this rule when instructing an agent. Beware of a random check of learned material: it can fade unchecked information out of memory.

★ Train your brain – Matches. Level 3

Don't forget to keep practicing with your matches! To remember the location of matches better, group them into geometric figures. Maybe the randomly spilled matches remind you of something? Use this image for memorization.

Do not give up if you cannot perform an exercise well. Keep on trying or come back to the previous level. Repeat the exercises regularly.

Zeigarnik effect

The Zeigarnik effect states that uncompleted or interrupted tasks are remembered better than completed tasks. Sitting in a cafe, psychologists Kurt Lewin and Blum Zeigarnik noticed that the waiter didn't write down their order, but fulfilled it exactly. When the waiter was then asked about the order of the visitors who had just left, he could not remember anything.

Subsequent experiments have shown that interrupted intellectual tasks are remembered twice as well as completed tasks. Perhaps this effect of incomplete action can be explained by preservation of motivational tension, which activates memory. The motivation disappears when the task is completed and a person forgets everything that was associated with the action.

The Zeigarnik effect is very useful in practice. For example, if you are writing a long text and stop in the middle of a chapter without finishing it, it will be easier for you to get back to work the next time. It will help you to recall where you've left off and what you wanted to write more easily and faster.

The effect of the unfinished action can be applied by interacting with other people. If you interrupt a conversation in the middle while tension is at its highest and without having drawn a conclusion, the impact on the interlocutor will be much stronger. They will look back on the issue, think about it and be more likely to agree with your point of view.

Test yourself

According to the KGB scientific consultant, what
is the main direction military psychologists
are taking in the field of suggestive techniques
improvement?

A) Removing doubt of the perceived information
   in a hypnotic trance

B) Removing pain in a hypnotic trance

C) Increasing people's physical strength in a
   hypnotic trance

D) The ability to hypnotize anyone without the
   help of the hypnotized

3
FREELANCE INTELLIGENCE OPERATIVE

Intelligence is not the main job of an agent. They are often in touch with other agents, giving them assignments, providing necessary equipment and valuable information. Meanwhile, an agent will live an ordinary life: working, meeting with friends while gathering information and performing intelligence tasks.

Forgetting

Forgetting is a very important function of memory. It protects the brain from an information overload.

Firstly, we forget excessive information that has not been used for a long time. This information is impossible and impractical to store in its original form, so the brain processes and generalizes it. Sometimes this sort of generalization takes the form of intuition – a feeling that cannot be explained logically. In this way, the brain gives us instinctive clues, building on the experience of similar situations we have actually forgotten.

Secondly, we forget any unpleasant information. Painful memories, such as the death of relatives or a dangerous accident or disaster, a crime, or an act that goes against one's values and beliefs, are unconsciously pushed out of the memory, restoring one's psychological comfort.

The act of forgetting is time-dependent: the more time that has passed from the moment the information was received, the higher the chance of forgetting. Long breaks from an intelligence operation can do a lot of harm to the case. Losing a sense of context might require an agent to start all over again.

However, a small pause of a week or two might be useful. It allows a broadening of perspective. Unimportant details and little things fade into the background, allowing for a more complete perception and the ability to look at the problem in a new way. Previously unnoticed patterns become apparent. New ideas form.

In psychology, there is a theory that a person cannot forget information once it is assimilated, but rather can lose access to it. Forgotten information doesn't disappear forever; in special circumstances, it can be recalled again. This is proven by an experiment involving neurosurgery, when stimulation of some areas of the cerebral cortex evokes forgotten memories.

But direct stimulation of the cortex is not the only way to recall something that has been forgotten. A few methods for recalling were mentioned earlier. The most important aspect of all of them is a mental reproduction of the situation in which the information was received.

Method of loci

The story method is not the only way to remember a list of words. The story is not important in itself – it is only a means of associating words, encoding them into images and placing them in emotionally tinged situations. Associativity, imagery and emotion, which are necessary for successful memorization, underlie one more method – the method of loci. The story method connects images with a storyline, the method of loci places them in a familiar location: in a house, in a room or on the street.

The method of loci originated in ancient history. There is a legend recounted by the Roman orator Marcus Tullius Cicero that the method of loci was invented by the Greek poet Simonides of Ceos, who lived in the fifth and sixth centuries BC. Simonides was at a feast when he was summoned by some unknown people. The poet went outside, and at this time the roof collapsed. All the other guests died. It was impossible to identify the bodies, but Simonides remembered every place at the table, and thus helped people to find the bodies of their relatives.

Cicero, who described this incident in his treatise 'On the Orator', concluded that in order to memorize a list of objects, it is necessary to form their mental images and place them in an imaginary location. The order of places will keep the order of memorized items.

Cicero himself used the method of loci when he memorized his speeches. Rehearsing the speech, he walked through his villa, and each room was associated with a particular topic or idea.

Another great example of using the method of loci is the 'Theatre of Memory' of Giulio Camillo. During the Renaissance, in the sixteenth century, this philosopher and alchemist attempted to create a comprehensive system of human knowledge, putting it in a special building – the theatre of memory. Each area of knowledge had its place there, all areas were linked, and compounded a complete picture. Camillo even started construction of a wooden building for the theatre, but did not complete it. He also didn't finish the fundamental work that described the theatre in detail. However, the idea of a visual representation of knowledge and links between its parts had a major impact on Camillo's contemporaries.

The art of memory has always been associated with government, international relations and intelligence services. Simonides of Ceos is known to have had political influence in Greece because of his poems about the Greek–Persian wars. In addition, he was a diplomat who resolved conflicts and prevented bloodshed. Cicero was a significant figure in Roman politics. His unique eloquence and memory gained him popularity and got him elected consul. Giulio Camillo's employer was Francis I, who ruled France for thirty years.

Aristotle, Seneca, Augustine of Hippo, Albert the Great, Thomas Aquinas, Giordano Bruno, René Descartes, Francis Bacon, Wilhelm Leibniz – this is a very incomplete list of famous people who have contributed to the theory and practice of memory. Each of them was an influential man of his day, and some of them were engaged in the intelligence service and espionage.

Method

It's best to begin mastering the method with a small, well-known place: say, the apartment you live in. Imagine it. Find areas (loci) where you can position and arrange various objects.

For example, there is an entrance hall, a living room, a hallway, a kitchen and a bathroom in your apartment. Mentally go round every room counter-clockwise. (If it's too difficult, actually go through the apartment and look carefully around the rooms.) Here's what you might notice:

1. Entrance hall:

a small bench;

a cupboard with three compartments;

a coat rack.

2. Living room:

a corner shelf;

two bookshelves;

a sofa;

a desk;

a windowsill;

a sideboard;

a painting hanging on a nail.

3. Hallway;

4. Kitchen:

cat's bowls on the floor;

a table;

a small sofa,

etc.

Thus, even in a small apartment it's easy to find twenty or thirty places where you can put items. Obviously, your apartment and the location of the items will be different, but the point is you should know them well.

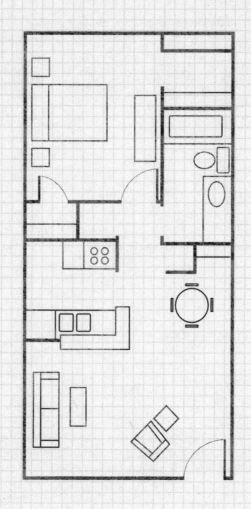

Here is a list of words you might recognize:

fireworks

orange

car

clock

sofa

painting

algebra

doctor

magazine

staff

skyscraper

meteorite

Here is how you can remember it:

You walk through the door and immediately see **fireworks**. Flaming Catherine wheels are attached to the bench in the hallway. They are whistling and spinning, scattering hot sparks. The hallway is filled with smoke and a strong smell of gunpowder. There is a bright juicy **orange** in the first compartment of the cupboard. It is so big that in order to put it into the cupboard, you had to squeeze it. The peel has split, smelly and sticky juice is flowing into the adjacent second compartment of the cupboard, where you can see a tiny **car.** The acidic orange juice is dripping onto the car, and its body is being covered with red spots of rust. A big wall **clock** is ticking in the third compartment of the cupboard. It measures out how much time the rapidly rusting car has left. There is a coat rack next to the cupboard and you can see a cosy green velvet **sofa** hanging on it. Carrying a sofa around is convenient. You always have a place to sit down when you are tired. But where can you leave a sofa? On the rack, of course.

You enter the living room. There is a corner shelf just past the door. You want to see if there is anything on it, but you cannot because it is completely covered with a large bright **painting**, hanging there for no good reason. You are trying to get to the shelf, but the painting is hammered in firmly. There is an **algebra** problem on the first bookshelf. Or rather, an interactive graph of a problem. The **Doctor** of Mathematics, sitting in the adjacent second bookshelf, is very happy about this, because he has been dreaming of studying this very function for so long. The scientist is thrilled. He's not going to part with the problem and will stay by this bookshelf for a long time. There is a big **magazine**, apparently brought in by the doctor, on the sofa. The magazine is huge and heavy. It is clear why the magazine is on the sofa: there is no room for it anywhere else. You can see it pressing into the sofa. How did the doctor even bring it here? The magazine **staff** are sitting on the desk. There is not enough space, and the whole group is crowded around, from the editor to the office boy hanging on to the edge of the desk, because he has been pushed aside by the loud journalistic fraternity arguing about something. On the windowsill next to the desk is a model of the **skyscraper** the magazine staff dream of moving into. But this skyscraper has such a bizarre shape that it seems it will never be built. Apparently, this group of staff is fated to wander other people's rooms. You notice something curious on the corner of the sideboard. It is a **meteorite**. Its surface is melted, rugged, ruddy with rust, and it resembles a building designed by Gaudi. It probably fell recently, because it's still hot and smells like a hot iron. Actually, that is the only interesting thing you can find in the apartment. It was brought here recently, and you stay at the sideboard, examining your discovery.

This picture seems absurd, strange and ridiculous, but that is what makes it good. It is easier to remember this way. The main thing is to place the listed items in a well-known space, one that is easily remembered. Please note the three main principles of mnemonics in the story.

1. **Associativity** – The objects are linked to a well-known place and sometimes to each other.

2. **Imagery** – All of the words are turned into bright images. They move, they make noise, they have weight, colour, taste, smell and texture.

3. **Emotion** – You are afraid of getting burnt by the fireworks; you want orange juice, but make a wry face when you imagine its sour taste and the way it sticks to the walls of the cupboard; you pity the rusting car; you are surprised at the man who keeps his sofa with him at all times. You are curious about what is behind the painting, and you worry about the doctor, who had to carry a heavy magazine.

Using the method of loci

In order to use the method of loci, you need to be very familiar with a location. You need to be able to navigate this place easily, to move mentally between rooms and to remember what comes next clearly. Specifically, it is not enough to remember that there is a wardrobe behind the door. You should be able to imagine everything about this wardrobe – its size, its shape, colour, the feeling of touching it, the creak of its door and the way it smells inside.

It is better to choose loci so that they are different from each other. Bookcases that are similar or that are standing side by side might cause interference in your memory, adding to the risk of confusing objects.

When mastering the method of loci, it's also better to choose real places, especially ones you can visit. Once you've mastered the method, to test yourself try using completely invented worlds. Make them memorable, think through all of the details. Come back to them often, and these imaginary places will serve you well.

Exercise

Pick three locations for using the method of loci. Mentally go round each of them, imagining every locus, every object. Everything in your location has a size, shape, colour, weight, texture and smell. Use it: move the imaginary furniture, knock on the table, open the door and touch the armrest.

After you have used places that actually exist, try creating a location using only your imagination.

Body memory

To remember short lists you can also use your parts of your body. Suppose you are preparing a public speech and you need to remember its outline. Place the image of the content of the first part of the speech on your feet and tie it to your shoes. The second part can be connected to your knee and the third part to your hip.

You can place no fewer than ten items on your body:

1. feet;

2. knees;

3. shins;

4. hips;

5. waist;

6. stomach;

7. chest;

8. shoulders;

9. neck;

10.head.

This memory technique will prevent you losing your train of thought when giving a presentation to colleagues and strangers.

★ Train your brain – Word list. Method of loci. Level 1

Master the method of loci in this simple exercise. When memorizing a list, mentally place the concepts in a familiar space. Try to use your body as a mnemonic space.

Notes

28 April 1955,
Moscow

In order to accelerate the operational investigation of
the missing RSHA documents, I advise investing the agent
'Simonides' with the authority of Operating Officer and allowing
him to communicate with recruited agents 'Archaeologist',
'Michael' and 'Rostovets'.

I also propose entrusting 'Simonides' with organizing the
set-up to identify the agent network interested in access to
psychological developments.

Chief Operating Officer
of the Second Main Directorate
Major I. O. Miloslavsky

★ Train your brain – Word list. Method of loci. Level 2

Master the skill of memorizing words by using the method of loci. This time, imagine the space of your room or apartment.

Notes

30 April 1955

Met with my handler yesterday. He told me I'd been promoted. Now I'm an intelligence operative, though freelance. This means I don't just collect information, I participate in operations, too. It also means that I have to be more careful.

April has been very full. More training. A break-up with Z. My first recruits. Kovalev's interrogation and death. A promotion. I can hardly imagine my past life anymore, when I would just serve out my hours at the dean's office. Now, every day is full of motion and meaning.

Story method and method of loci

You already know two methods for memorizing lists: the story method and the method of loci. They have a lot in common, and above all both of them satisfy the three basic principles of mnemonics: associativity, imagery and emotion. But there are differences: in the story method, associations are built from object to object, in the loci method, they are built from the object to its place in an imaginary location.

It is better to be able to use both methods. Perhaps you will choose one of them, or maybe you will use each one for different tasks, it's up to you to decide. Each method has its advantages and disadvantages.

An important advantage of the method of loci is that you do not need to recall the whole story to find an object from a memorized list. For example, if you needed to find the fifth object from our earlier list, in your imagination you would immediately go to the coat rack and see the sofa.

The limitations of the method of loci are also obvious. First, you need to imagine a large space to remember a long list. Second, you need to have a lot of familiar spaces so as not to mix up different lists. This is its main limitation, but some people still like it more than the story method.

At the same time, the same space can be reused. Once a memorized list is no longer relevant, you can mentally go around your space and empty it by removing the images. Go around once more and make sure that there is nothing left. Now it can be used again.

★ Train your brain – Word dictation. Method of loci. Level 2

Using the method of flicking through a book and picking nouns from the top left of each page, keep memorizing words. The method of loci is often more convenient and efficient than the story method.

Exercise

Remember some lists of words using one of the different methods.
Determine the most effective method for you.

List 1:

coffee

sea

screen

door

crane

horse

thunder

thrush

end

myth

List 2:

refrigerator

interpolation

suffix

trammel

surprise

navigation

symmetry

ferris wheel

luminescence

creativity

AGENT REPORT

- -
Re: Case #283
April 30, 1955
Source: 'Simonides'
Received by: Major I. O. Miloslavsky
- -

On Kovalev's contacts

The survey of Kovalev's friends on his connections with
foreign residents revealed that:

Kovalev was well acquainted with François Legly, the son of
the Adviser on Culture to the French Embassy to the Soviet
Union, Jean Legly.

In addition, there is evidence that in the Hermitage in
Leningrad, Kovalev became acquainted with an unknown
foreign art enthusiast. They met several times.

Some books of Italian art in Spanish that were never sold
in the USSR were found in Kovalev's room.

#215

1 May 1955

We're working on two foreigners right now. Frenchmen.
A father and son. It's astonishing how different they
are, how unlike Soviets they are in their behaviour
and mannerisms. Especially the elder. Although, it
could be a quirk of diplomatic service — emanating
polish and self-confidence. Status. I wonder what
he'll look like if they catch him spying red-handed.
I've heard that diplomats don't get prosecuted, only
deported. But the residents are still afraid. There's
nothing to look forward to at home if the KGB
uncovers them.

Test Yourself

Write down the code names of the three agents recruited by Simonides to help in the mission to find the missing documents.

★ Train your brain – Word list. Level 3

Now that you've mastered the story method and the method of loci, keep improving them. Memorize longer lists, reducing the time allotted. Alternate methods after every three or four lists.

3 May 1955, Moscow

Memo from the investigation of
François Legly

Case # 283

CONFIDENTIAL

François Legly, son of the Adviser on Culture to the French
Embassy to the Soviet Union, Jean Legly, b. 1933. Resides
on the territory of the French Embassy in Moscow. Does not
have diplomatic immunity.

Information exists about the connection between the
cultural adviser and the French intelligence service. It
is possible that under diplomatic cover he is the head of
the French agency resident in Moscow. Such cases of using
residents' family members for connections with foreign
intelligence agents have been reported, so François Legly
has been put under surveillance (object 'Dandy').

François Legly has a very wide circle of friends. In the
reports from agents of the Seventh Division there is
information about meetings between Kovalev and Legly in
Dzerzhinsky Square and in Kirov Street and about their
walks through Moscow, during which they exchanged large
paper bags and bundles. Their meetings did not look
secretive. They did not attempt to escape from agents, nor
was there any counter-surveillance.

To avoid conflicts with the embassy, no action has been
taken towards François Legly's connections.

Chief Operating Officer
of the Second Main Directorate
Major I. O. Miloslavsky

★ Train your brain – Word dictation. Level 3

Alternate using the story method and the method of loci when memorizing lists of words. This time try to spend only three seconds on each word.

10 May 1955

The case of the missing archival documents has hit a dead end. At least for me. Kovalev is dead. Bernstein probably is, too. The Frenchmen, I think, have absolutely no interest in investigating Nazi psychopaths. Although I understand that not all cases get solved, I really don't want my first case to remain unsolved.

Keeping my chin up.

Figures and numbers

Most people find remembering numbers difficult. Perhaps because numbers are the most abstract information, much less tangible and real than words and names. To make numbers more specific, and therefore easier to remember, you can encode them into images. To start, picture images for single-digit numbers. Then move on to create a set of images for two- or even three-digit numbers. Usually someone else's system for memorizing numbers is of little use, so when you become an experienced mnemonist, you can create your own.

Numbers can be encoded in different ways. One option is to use the resemblance of numbers to images and objects. For example:

```
0 - a ball, a hat, a ring

1 - a candle, a spear, a feather

2 - a swan, a crawling snail, a desk-lamp

3 - a moustache, a cloud, a camel (if you turn them
    sideways)

4 - a chair, a sailing boat, a weather vane

5 - a crane hook, a ladle, palm tree

6 - a rolled elephant's trunk, a wheelbarrow with one
    wheel, a watermelon with a stalk

7 - a door handle, a desk-lamp post, a golf club

8 - glasses, an hourglass, a bicycle

9 - a balloon with a rope, a monocle with a chain, a
    lollipop
```

Another option for coding digits is using rhyme or similar sounds:

0 - hero, mirror

1 - gun, fun, sun

2 - tooth, glue, clue

3 - tree, tea, degree

4 - door, store, war

5 - wife, live, dive

6 - sticks, ships, eclipse

7 - heaven, servant, sever

8 - gate, skate, aid

9 - night, fine, wine

You can even encode digits with fictional characters:

0 - Zorro

1 - One Hundred and One Dalmatians

2 - The Two Ronnies

3 - The Three Musketeers

4 - The Four Horsemen of the Apocalypse

5 - Captain Planet's Planeteers

6 - The Bionic Six

7 - The Seven Dwarfs

8 - Sleeping Beauty ('8' is similar to a woman's shape)

9 - The Fellowship of the Ring

You can use an existing system or come up with a more suitable one for you. The main thing is that the images in this system are specific, easy to visualize and clear to you. It is also better when images are not similar to one another otherwise they can cause interference.

To remember any sequence of numbers, all you have to do is imagine a story about it, encoding each digit with an image. Let's suppose that your phone number is 120-1580. Here is a story that can help you remember this phone number: A feather (1) is whirling slowly in the wind. It fell from a flying white swan (2) in a black hat (0). The swan holds a burning candle (1) in one leg, shielding it from the oncoming air stream with a ladle (5). An hourglass (8) is attached to the ladle handle and it measures out the time that it takes the swan to fly around a circle (0).

Here is another example. Let's suppose that you need to remember your credit card PIN, 4837. You can invent the following story. A sailing boat (4) is sailing on the sea. The sea is calm and so the sailors have attached bike wheels (8) to the boat and they are turning the pedals as hard as they can to make it move faster. But there is a cloud (3) with a door handle (7) floating by in the sky. They don't have to turn the pedals any more, they can just grab on to the handle.

The technique of memorizing numbers through image substitution is based on the same universal principles of mnemonics: abstract digits are encoded into visual images, the images are then linked to each other through a story and the absurdity of the story makes them easier to remember.

Learning to memorize numbers is a bit more difficult than learning to memorize words. Nevertheless, it is possible. Mnemonists like to set records in memorizing pi. The current Guinness World Record for this is well in excess of 60,000 digits.

Exercise

Remember your personal numerical information: the PINs of your bank cards, document numbers, phone numbers of your family and friends and their dates of birth, etc.

Exercise

As we know, the most reliable computer passwords contain letters, numbers and special characters. Create and memorize a few complex passwords, protecting your data. The letters can be coded with words, each word beginning with a specific password letter. Special characters can be coded with the items they are similar to: @ is a dog with a long tail or a cat curled up in a ball; # is bars on a window, $ is a dollar, a coin or a note; % is a face (eyes with a long nose between them); ^ is a house, a roof, etc.

For example, if your password is 'r45^hlm'. The story can be this: a rat (r) is dragging a sailing boat (4) that has a huge ladle (5) instead of a rudder. The boat has a little roof (^) made of hops (h). There are some lions (l) on the roof picking the hop cones off the stems and throwing them to the deck for monkeys (m) to pick up.

The more you remember and the more often you make up these stories, the faster you learn to do so quickly and easily.

15 May 1955

Our training is more fun than the circus, sometimes. We can spend two hours talking to someone without saying anything about ourselves. We can get the most private people to open up and tell us what we need and we can read between the lines. We can completely confuse someone or make them pay attention to something specific. Here's one of our assignments: spend all day going around town in taxis, and in the evening, report everything about the drivers: their names and last names, where they were born, where they live, whether they have families, how old their kids are and how they like their work. The key is to find someone's 'pet topic', and then he's yours. It's harder to extract yourself from that sort of conversation than to strike it up.

But hypnosis . . . that's something else entirely. There was a demonstration at school today. One of the students, K., was hypnotized and interrogated. We learned a lot of interesting things about him and about ourselves. Although we, the students, barely talk to each other about anything outside of training itself. I wonder if he'll remember what he said. I've heard some do.

We didn't see the hypnotist, because his identity was being kept secret; we only heard him. (I wonder if K. saw him.) However, his words affected me from behind the thick screen. They affected other people too, from what I could tell. Fascinating. And frightening. I wouldn't want to be interrogated like that.

★ Train your brain – Map. Level 1

Look at a map in a book or on the Internet. Create a simple route for yourself, taking note of the streets and roads. Put the map away and give yourself a couple of minutes to write down the directions for the route you created. Remember it and select the right streets on the map. Imagine yourself walking down the street. What can you see to your right and left? At what street will you turn?

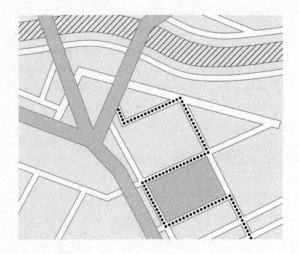

<u>SURVEILLANCE RESULTS FOR THE 'DANDY'</u>

16 May 1955,
Moscow

On 5 May the target met with MSU student Privalov, E. F.
(b. 1935), on 7 May he met with MIPT students Grigoriev,
M. R. (b. 1935), and Lukin, V. L. (b. 1935) and on 8 May
— with the IISS student Fomin, A. A. (b. 1933). These
meetings took place on benches in Gorky Park, Neskuchny
Garden, December Uprising Park. In all cases, 'Dandy'
handed over bulky packages and bundles.

Further surveillance of people who met with 'Dandy'
shows that they returned to their places of residence.
No counter-surveillance was noted, no attempts to escape
surveillance were made.

The Seventh Division staff conducted interviews with people
who met with 'Dandy'. They did not cooperate, and said
that they had seen 'Dandy' for the first time and had not
received anything from him. Thus, the purpose of the
meetings was not determined.

I consider it appropriate to continue surveillance on the
target.

Chief Operating Officer
of the Seventh Main Directorate
Captain M. V. Kozmin

#102a

16 May 1955,
Moscow

<u>Results of the investigation</u>
<u>on S. Y. Bernstein</u>
(Case #283)

There are no results on the investigation of S. Y.
Bernstein (b. 1897), who disappeared in February 1955.
Bernstein's relatives and friends were examined. Because of
the possibility that Bernstein is using false documents,
an investigation was made of everyone newly registered
in Moscow and Leningrad in the period from the end of
February 1955 to the present. Nobody matching Bernstein's
description was found.

                                    Chief Operating Officer
                        of the Second Main Directorate
                                    Major I. O. Miloslavsky

17 May 1955,
Moscow

<u>On the detention of a foreign citizen</u>
<u>François Legly</u>
(Case #283)

Surveillance reports conducted by Seventh Directorate
agents have substantiated the suspicion that a citizen
of France, François Legly, is a courier for communication
between the French residency and agents. The decision
was made to detain François Legly during a transfer of
instructions or equipment to a probable agent.

On 17 May at 18:30 François Legly left the territory of the
embassy and went to Neskuchny Garden with a bundle wrapped
in newspaper. At 19:05, he sat down on a bench near the
entrance to the park on which Lukin, V. L. (b. 1935), a
second-year MIPT student was sitting. During the transfer
of the bundle, both were detained by operatives of the
Second Chief Directorate.

There were French records in the bundle. Lukin showed that
he was buying 'jazz' records from François Legly. These
records are not sold in Moscow. Lukin paid to Legly 20 to
50 roubles per record.

Chief Operating Officer
of the Second Main Directorate
Major I. O. Miloslavsky

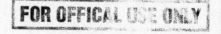

18 May 1955,
Moscow

On the investigation of
the missing classified documents
(file with Case #283)

The French Ministry of Foreign Affairs sent a statement
of protest to the Foreign Ministry in response to the
unfounded detention of a French citizen, François Legly,
on 17 May 1955.

I place a demerit on the record of all members of the
group investigating missing classified RSHA documents
and of the Chief Operating Officer of the Second Main
Directorate Major I. O. Miloslavsky for their mistakes
and lack of attention in their performance.

Deputy Chief
of the Second Main Directorate
Colonel V. I. Rukin

★ Train your brain – Letter pairs, 6×5

Pick fifteen pairs of letter tiles and arrange them in six rows of five. Turn over the tiles, trying to find matching pairs of letters. Try not to turn over the same tile twice. Trust your memory.

Notes

Memorization and recognition

The only way to make sure that you have remembered something is to reproduce it in full without any help or prompting, and then compare it with the original material. Not to feel that you know it, not to remember something in the story of another person or in the text, but to write it down and compare it. This rule is used firmly in intelligence services when something must be learned: an instruction or a cover story. Everything is checked through complete recall.

Why is this so important? Certainly there have been situations in your life, such as preparing for exams, when you thought that you knew the material well and could definitely reproduce it, but then during the exam you could not recall it. The fact is that the ability to recognize information, and the subjective feeling that you have learned it, comes much sooner than actual memorization. The fact that you can recognize material in a book does not mean that you'll be able to recall it when you need to.

Are you giving instructions to an agent? Ask him to repeat the instructions. If you tell him the sequence of actions, they should repeat it in both forward and reverse order. Are you preparing for an exam? Recall the material and write it down on a piece of paper. The subjective sensation of remembering and recognizing is not enough. And keep in mind one of the laws of memory: partial reproduction makes memorized information worse, it is better to recall all of it.

Professional memory

Perhaps you've noticed that football fans remember a huge amount of information. Before an important match a true fan predicts its result, and this prediction is often well founded. Fans will remember the outcomes of matches of the same teams under similar conditions, the statistics of key players, decisive goals, referees' mistakes, etc. The day after a match, a fan can talk about the game for two hours, discussing every nuance, every play.

Fans are not the only ones with great memories. The same can be said of collectors, movie buffs and scientists. All of them remember a lot of facts, dates, numbers, attributes, cases and descriptions. It has to be said that true enthusiasts rarely memorize all this information intentionally. They learn it easily and effortlessly.

In addition to the high level of motivation that professionals have, this can also be explained by their extensive network of associations. Each new event, new fact or new number is associated with familiar information: this runner improved his record by so many milliseconds, this team won for the first time in this season, etc. The brain easily remembers something it is accustomed to, something that is emotionally coloured and meaningful. This is how long-time fans often quite accurately predict match results, though it's impossible for them to explain how they came up with the forecast.

Of course, intelligence officers have phenomenal memory and sensitive intuitions. Because intelligence work is not just a job, it is a way of life and life and death itself.

Test yourself

Who was responsible for organizing the set-up to identify the agent network interested in access to psychological developments of the RSHA?

A) Major Miloslavsky

B) Agent 'Michael'

C) Agent 'Simonides'

D) Colonel Rukin

4
SHUTTLE
AGENT

Some operations require the direct presence of a scout in another country. To perform assignments 'on the road', the agent must have not only special knowledge but also the necessary connections.

Shuttle agents therefore often leave knowledge, connections and most importantly reliable cover information for other operational staff. The work of a shuttle agent abroad is dangerous, but working under the observation of the enemy's special services requires true skill.

19 May 1955,
Moscow

<u>On Kovalev's connections</u>
(file with Case #283)

With the support of the USSR Ministry of Foreign Affairs,
an informal meeting was held with the Adviser on Culture
to the French Embassy to the Soviet Union, Jean Legly
(the father of François Legly). A private apology was
made to Mr Legly and an explanation of the reasons for
his son's detention was given.

Over the course of the interview, a personal connection
was established with Jean Legly on the basis of
a discussion about children of the same age and
their behaviour. He responded to the incident with
understanding and admitted that François's actions may
have legitimately aroused the suspicions of Soviet state
security. He also said that he was dissatisfied with his
son's behaviour in the Soviet Union and intended to
send him back to France.

Having learned that the detention was connected to
Kovalev's death, the adviser said, 'He should not have
fallen in with that crazy Argentinian.'

He also said that, according to his son, Kovalev
sometimes interacted with Mr Alvarez, a strange man
from Latin America, an art historian who was often in
the USSR. Mr Legly expressed concern that Alvarez might
be involved in something illegal. He advised his son to
stay away from both Alvarez and Kovalev.

Deputy Chief
of the Second Main Directorate
Colonel V. I. Rukin

Presentations and speeches

Nothing is more depressing than a speech that is read from the page. You can hardly justify such disregard for the audience by asserting that public speaking is stressful for the speaker. Fear of public speaking is high on the list of phobias that affect people. Orators were among the first people to use mnemonic techniques. If there is no need to check the next sentence on a piece of paper, the orator can be more confident and deal with his stress better.

There is no need to memorize a speech word for word for a good performance. It's enough just to remember the main points and the links between them. This way you will not forget your lines and you will still leave space for improvisation and live communication with the audience.

1. Divide your speech into semantic units. There is no need to make it too small; it's enough to have 5–10 units for a small speech.

2. Formulate the thesis (main idea of each block) – make it a sentence of three or four words.

3. Encode every thesis with a single key word that can clearly define the statement.

4. Remember the list of key words using the story or loci method. You can use your body as a mnemonic space.

5. Rehearse your presentation. Retell or write down the thesis of your speech, reproducing key words from memory. Repeat them in order and in reverse.

Stage actors memorize long texts word for word, and their experience can be very useful. Preparing for a play does not begin with memorizing phrases, but with understanding the characters' feelings as they change with the development of the plot. Once an actor gets into the essence of his or her hero, the text becomes clear, logical and can be remembered faster and better.

Think about the feelings you want to provoke in your listeners at every point of your speech. Live these emotions and put them into words.

Exercise

Read a short article. Divide it into semantic units. Write down the main ideas of these units using theses. Define the key words and memorize them. Try to retell the article, and then check your story with the original text.

Do this exercise using articles on different subjects. This not only develops memory but also the ability to capture, process and compress information. The ability to present the most important part of a large volume of extracted information in a short report is extremely valuable for an intelligence officer.

Memorizing and structure

To remember a large amount of information better, organize it. One of the most effective ways to organize disparate data is to classify it using a tree structure.

For example, you need to remember the objects on your desk. Perhaps to make sure nobody was looking through your office in your absence. The following objects are on your desk:

a laptop;

a fountain pen;

a notebook (with a bookmark on the 15th page);

several blank sheets of paper;

a pencil sharpener;

a detector for finding listening devices;

last year's copy of *Countries of the World*;

an external hard drive;

a framed photo;

a memory card;

a statue of the Buddha;

a pencil;

a book on the psychology of emotions;

a phone charger.

It's not very easy to remember the list in its original form. But you can classify the objects. For example, you can divide them into electronic devices and everything else. The list will be as follows:

1. Electronic devices:

   a laptop;

   a detector for finding listening devices;

   an external hard drive;

   a memory card;

   a phone charger.

2. The rest:

   a fountain pen;

   a notebook (with a bookmark on the 15th page);

   several blank sheets of paper;

   a pencil sharpener;

   last year's copy of *Countries of the World*;

   a framed photo;

   a statue of the Buddha;

   a pencil;

   a book on the psychology of emotions.

The list is clearer, but the groups are still too large. You can divide them into sub-groups:

1. Electronic devices:

A)   Data storage devices:

        a laptop;

        an external hard drive;

        a memory card.

B)   Other devices:

        a detector for finding listening devices;

        a phone charger.

2. The rest:

A)   Writing materials:

        a fountain pen;

        a notebook (with a bookmark on the 15th page);

        several blank sheets of paper;

        a pencil sharpener;

        a pencil;

B)   Books:

        last year's copy of *Countries of the World*;

        book on the psychology of emotions.

C)   Decorations:

        statue of the Buddha;

        a framed photo.

Now you have a two-level classification tree.

The construction of such a tree takes some time. However, experiments show that ordered information is remembered up to ten times more effectively than a simple list.

Make sense of your information, build charts and tables, classify and organize it.

Test Yourself

In the 'Figures and Numbers' exercise, what film represents the number 9?

A) District 9

B) The Fellowship of the Ring

C) Finding Nemo

D) The Goonies

Mind maps

For a visual representation of data structure, you can use mind mapping, a technique developed by British psychologist Tony Buzan. Incidentally, he is a founder of memory championships, where the world's best mnemonists compete in remembering and accurately reproducing all sorts of different information.

Mind maps are indispensable when you need to master a new area of knowledge quickly. You can link fragmented information together and find connections between seemingly independent facts.

To make a mind map, do the following:

1.   Take a blank sheet of paper. Turn it horizontally.

2.   Indicate the main topic of your mind map in the centre of the page.
     It can be a picture, a word or a phrase – anything you want. The
     main thing is that you should understand and remember it.

3.   Expand and clarify the main topic. Draw lines from the main topic and
     label them with explanatory key words or pictures.

Think about cause and effect. What affects the topic of your map? Where might it lead? What dangers might it present? What components does it consist of? The questions will depend on the topic of the map, and there can be many of them. Don't let that put you off. It is possible that as you develop the map, some lines will come together, and some lines will be left blank.

4.   Do the same thing with each line: explain each one as a separate topic.
     From the end of each line, draw new branches and mark them with key
     words or images.

5.   Continue branching from the centre to the periphery, until all your ideas
     appear on the map.

To make the map more useful, follow these recommendations:

1. It's better to encode ideas and words with images, even if you are not very good at drawing. You will remember them better this way.

2. If you use words, write a single word for one concept. Otherwise you map will be cumbersome and confusing.

3. Make words and images smaller and lines thinner the farther from the centre you get. It will show the hierarchy of knowledge and separate the most important information from the least important.

4. Use different colours.

5. Connect related concepts with lines and arrows or combine them into blocks.

6. Try not to make more than seven branches for each concept. If you need more, create another level of hierarchy.

A completed mind map looks like a neuron: a large image in the centre with a lot of tree-like branches. For example, there is a mind map overleaf illustrating the three principles of mnemonics.

The advantage of a mind map is that it is easily observable – all of the information is presented on a single page. The structure of the information and the connections between its elements are easily visible. The map itself corresponds with all three principles of mnemonics: associativity (all data are connected); imagery (information is presented visually), emotionality (colours, shadings and the character of the map reflect the author's attitude).

P.S. Maintain secrecy. Do not forget to destroy your mind maps after memorizing their contents.

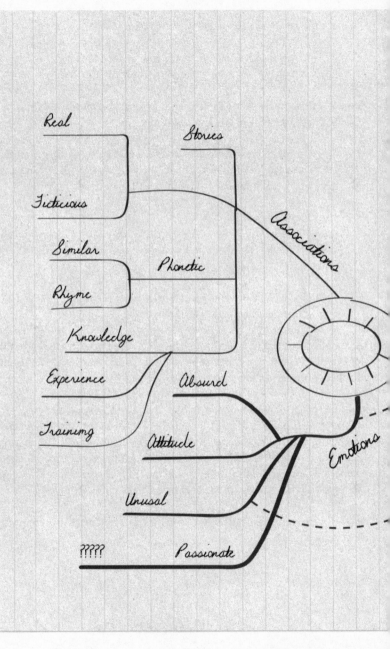

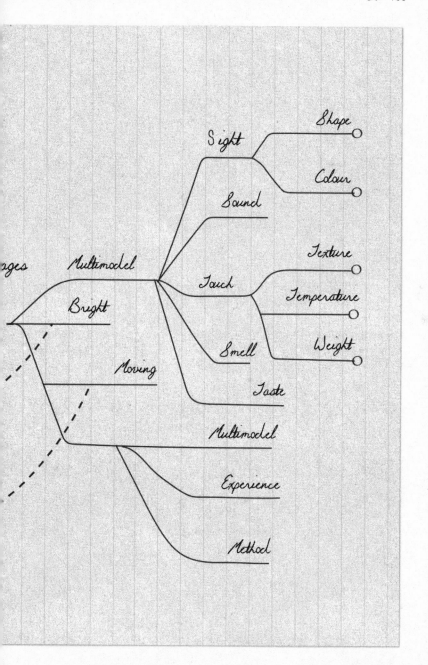

Exercise

Using a mind map, describe yesterday and tomorrow. The size of the map's elements will reflect time consumption, and the colour will indicate the importance of a particular task.

Notes

23 May 1955,
Moscow

<u>From the case file of operating investigation</u>
<u>of Argentine citizen Jose Alvarez</u>
(Case #283)

Photos of Kovalev and Jose Alvarez have been shown to
waiters in restaurants within a 20-minute drive from
the Philosophy Department building of MSU. Both were
recognized by E. P. Duzhkov, a waiter at Kolos, who was
working on 21 April, the day of Kovalev's death. They
split a bottle of wine. Only the younger one ate. The
foreigner paid.

Duzhkov remembered them well: the younger one looked
worried, was nervous and tried to leave. The foreigner
was soothing him and coaxing him to stay.

Chief Operating Officer
of the Second Main Directorate
Major I. O. Miloslavsky

2. July 1955

Buenos Aires. Would never have thought life could take me so far so quickly.

Feathers were pretty ruffled at the dean's office when they heard I was being sent to the psychology conference.

I've never written articles so fast. To be honest, though, the KGb archives are a treasure trove for a psychology historian. My report was approved. My paperwork was filed quickly. My instructions were thorough and took a long time to go through. Local counter-intelligence will probably be watching us, so I should be especially careful.

The timing's off, though. June—July is winter in Argentina. It's around 11 degrees over here. The beaches are empty. It's probably warmer in Moscow right now.

The class inequality is obvious here. For our own safety, we were advised to avoid the Argentinian poor. Even without the warning, I wouldn't want to get too close to them.

Just a few weeks ago, they almost had a revolution. The Catholics, Peron, unions, the military. I don't know the details, but it all ended in the bombing of the president's castle by the Argentinian air force, the head of which, as far as I can tell, joined the rebellion. The number of dead and wounded is not being reported. What's left of bombshells and explosions are all over the streets, and its pretty gruesome. You can see people crossing themselves when they pass certain areas. Some pray, falling on their knees and crying. That definitely sets them apart from the faithful in Moscow, who even if they do cross themselves, do it furtively, so no one sees.

How could they have even let us into the country at a time like this?! As far as I can tell, Perón won't stay in his position for long.

The Spanish isn't easy. The stuff I learned is very different from how they speak here. And the speed! And intonations!!! At first, I couldn't understand half of what anyone was saying, but now I've figured it out, and can sort of communicate with the locals. A different country, a different language and a different culture all force the brain to work at full capacity. There are a lot of foreigners here, but I have to learn to fit in, not to stand out. This takes work, being extra observant and paying attention to details. I fall into bed every night and pass out right away.

11 July 1955

I've got used to things here. The culture shock has passed. Work isn't letting me relax too much. Data collection on Alvarez is moving forward bit by bit. The Argentinians are a lot more open than the Russians. Or maybe I've got more experienced at asking questions and communicating with people.

The police were a bit harder to deal with. But not as hard as I thought they would be. Money buys you anything you want around here.

AGENT REPORT

- -

Re: Case #283
2 June 1955
Source: 'Simonides'
Received by: Major I. O. Miloslavsky

- -

On the last weeks of Kovalev's life

Questioning of Kovalev's neighbours indicate that he
behaved unusually in the last two months before his
death. During the Soviet Army Day celebration, he was 'as
if under a cloud' and had been depressed and looked ill
since then. He avoided contact. He almost stopped working
on his thesis, although he had put a lot of time into it
before.

Usually, Kovalev worked in the Archives three days
a week. After 23 February, he stopped going to the
Archives.

There is reason to believe that Kovalev knew about
Bernstein's disappearance before 2 March, when the police
received a report about it.

#479

★ Train your brain – Map. Level 2

Create a longer route to memorize from a different map. To help, it can be an area you are more familiar with. Give yourself one minute to write down the directions. Walk along the streets marked on the map, imagining the houses to your right and left, the parks, ponds, canals. Stop at the intersection, turn into the lane. Remember your impressions of what you have seen.

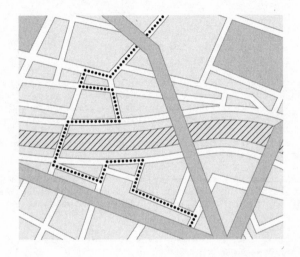

CIPHERED MESSAGE

-
Re: Case #283
13 July 1955
Source: 'Simonides'
Received by: Major I. O. Miloslavsky
- -

On Jose Alvarez

Jose Alvarez — Argentine citizen, b. 1907.
Lives in Buenos Aires.

Writes articles on art for several magazines in Latin America
and Europe. Teaches. Often travels for business. Interacts
with the museum staff, art historians, collectors and art
enthusiasts. Does not have diplomatic immunity.

Speaks English, German, Spanish and French. Can communicate in
Russian passably.

Connects with people easily. Joker with a good sense of
humour. Avid photographer. Takes many photos and gives them
out to acquaintances, establishing and developing personal
contacts.

Familiar with well-known artists, Pablo Picasso, Salvador
Dali, Joan Miró and others.

Often goes to the Soviet Union, especially to Moscow and
Leningrad. Has many friends among museum staff.

According to his friends, Alvarez's background is quite
ordinary. Spent almost his entire life in Argentina and only
began to travel outside the country in recent years. However,
this information requires verification, because none of those
questioned have known him for longer than one or two years.

Police sources in Argentina have informed us that art is
Alvarez's second profession, once a hobby. Before and during
the war, Alvarez worked as a travelling salesman for a small
company producing sewing machines.

From 14 January to 23 April 1955, Jose Alvarez was in Moscow.
The stated goal of his visit to the Soviet Union was working
with Lenin Library resources to write about Russian art. Went
to Leningrad several times.

Buenos Aires
#418

CIPHERED MESSAGE

- -

Re: Case #283
25 July 1955
Source: 'Simonides'
Received by: Major I. O. Miloslavsky

CONFIDENTIAL -

Report on the set-up organized
under the cover of the access to
classified documents

Attended the International Congress of Psychologists,
held in Buenos Aires on 18-22 July. Presented a report
on 'Exposing the anti-scientific theories of Nazi
psychologists in 1936-1945' on behalf of MSU in the
'History of Psychology' section. Referred to archives of
research organizations and universities.

The presentation garnered no additional questions, but
during the break a few members of the Congress expressed
interest in the stated subject. All of them were
scientists or lecturers. A list of their names and titles
is attached.

In accordance with the prepared cover, I made an offer of
collaboration to each person who approached me to work
in the field of history of psychology in Nazi Germany.
Two instructors expressed a willingness to travel to the
USSR for this purpose: Dracula Radu from Romania and Jose
Alvarez from Argentina.

The latter is not a professional psychologist. He is an
art historian, teaches art theory at several universities
in Latin America and France. Interested in the history of
psychology for a book he is writing on the specifics of
artistic perceptions of painting. Is in the USSR often.
In early October, will visit Moscow for an exhibition of
Latin American native painting.

Buenos Aires
#378

★ Train your brain – Word list. Level 4

Skills in memorizing words help in the preparation of speeches and allow one to better absorb what one has read. In addition, by practising memorizing lists, you improve your attention and imagination. The ability to quickly visualize words and concepts enhances your memory and enriches your thinking.

See if you can memorize word lists of ten words regularly, using the story method and the method of loci, alternating methods after every two or three lists.

Lifestyle and memory

The day-to-day lives of intelligence officers are a far cry from the textbook recommendations on healthy living. Psychological stress and lack of rest do not improve performance. Thrill-seeking intelligence officers with a tendency towards undue risk may have additional challenges.

Intelligence agencies do not encourage disregarding health and, especially, safety: employee training takes a long time and officers have a lot of important contacts. There are a lot of recommendations for making the professional life of an intelligence officer longer.

What can be done to maintain high performance and productivity? There are several aspects:

- proper nutrition;

- physical activity;

- optimal schedule;

- emotional health and reducing long-term stress.

These recommendations will be described in detail in the following sections.

★ Train your brain – Schulte Tables, 7×7

Below is a more complicated version of the Schulte Tables, containing 49 cells. Try to complete the exercise as quickly as possible, without moving your eyes from the middle cell. The 7×7 playing field is rather large, so this exercise challenges the outer boundaries of your peripheral vision capabilities.

35	39	32	28	5	23	22
16	2	44	12	42	3	30
7	36	9	10	33	24	48
11	13	38	4	26	47	45
19	43	34	46	49	37	15
8	1	41	6	14	40	25
21	18	27	31	29	20	17

Nutrition for the brain

The human brain makes up only 2% of the weight of the body, but it consumes about 20% of its energy. To maintain high-level performance of the nervous system, your diet must include:

- protein (yogurt, nuts, eggs, fish);

- complex carbohydrates (wholewheat bread, wholegrain cereals, durum wheat pasta);

- healthy fats (seafood, extra virgin olive oil, salmon, sardines, herring, avocados).

Proteins are essential for any living organism. Their deficiency causes fatigue and slows down the process of recovery.

Carbohydrates provide energy for the brain but should not be consumed in large amounts. Carbohydrates begin to raise blood glucose within a few minutes of sugar intake. The release of insulin reduces blood glucose levels, and the brain's nutrition problem still remains unsolved. It's far better to eat food with 'slow' carbohydrates: crusty bread, brown rice, beans, etc. These carbohydrates release their glucose into the blood slowly, so it is better absorbed and feeds the brain for a long time.

Since 60% of your brain matter consists of fats, do not try to eliminate all fats from your diet. Of course, not all fatty food is useful. Hydrogenated fats like margarine are bad for nerve cells, because they prevent the removal of waste products. Try not to eat foods containing vegetable fat. Unrefined vegetable oils, however, are useful. They clean the blood vessels and improve blood circulation.

One important biological function of the brain is to help us search for food. Brain activity depends on how hungry a person is. With a full stomach, brain activity slows down, causing drowsiness. Before you take on an important task, do not have a large meal, because mild hunger stimulates mental activity.

There is a lot of debate about the benefits and dangers of stimulants such as coffee and tea. Of course, a cup of coffee revives and improves mental ability, but long-term usage of large amounts of coffee leads to addiction and has harmful side effects. Perhaps the wisest advice in using natural stimulants is to practise moderation.

Drink plenty of fluids. Dehydration drastically reduces mental and physical performance.

Test Yourself

What is the name of the British psychologist who invented mind maps?

A) Miles Hewstone

B) Michael Rutter

C) Tony Buzan

D) Alexander Haslam

Physical activity

The value of physical activity for mental health is widely recognized. It contributes to well-being, improves blood flow and strengthens blood vessels, keeping them elastic. Regular exercise improves the functioning of the endocrine system and mitigates the emotional state, relieving stress. All of these benefits have a positive effect on mental performance. Complex movement also trains mind and memory. The association cortex of the brain, responsible for a person's cognitive abilities, is located next to the motor cortex that controls the contraction and relaxation of muscles. Motor cortex stimulation activates the association cortex, so movement makes us smarter. It is especially noticeable with children – motor skill development usually correlates with intellectual growth.

Physical activity invigorates. If you are overcome by drowsiness, do some exercise: turn your head, do a couple of arm swings, a dozen knee-bends or push-ups. If you reach an impasse in solving a complex problem, just go for a walk. While the consciousness will stop usual thinking, the subconscious keeps on searching for solutions. Unexpected associations and new ideas emerge.

There is a method that will be familiar to martial arts fans, that helps to quickly invigorate the mind and body. Stand up. Take a deep breath, slowly raising your hands, then exhale and quickly bring your hands down, sucking your stomach in. Blood will move from the internal organs to the limbs and the head; oxygen and nutrients will be brought to the brain.

Schedule and memory

When planning your day, consider the individual rhythm of your body. Some psychologists argue that the natural circadian rhythm of all people is about the same. In the morning, after sleeping, activity is high and in the evening it drops. However, breaking from a natural cycle, such as waking up later and staying awake past midnight, leads to a shift of activity to evening and night. 'Morning' people with a modified circadian rhythm become 'night' people. Even if you are used to being a night person, experiment with your schedule. Maybe the morning hours will be more productive for you.

To avoid getting out of the natural rhythm of your body, do not deviate from your usual schedule over the weekend. When there is no need to get up early the next morning, the temptation to stay up late is strong. Try to resist it. You may run the risk of missing the most productive hours of your personal time!

Studies of the circadian rhythm of a large sample of people shows that the mental capacity of a human reaches a maximum in the morning from about 8 to 12 o'clock. After lunch, it falls off steeply, then it gradually grows and falls again in the evening. This pattern is typical for most people, but others may have their own individual characteristics. The best way to know your circadian rhythm is by observation and experimentation.

Sleep greatly affects health, performance and psychological state. A sleep-deprived person can have difficulty controlling behaviour and emotional responses. They become irritable and less reasonable, making more mistakes.

The ability to remember also depends on sleep quality. There is a theory that the processing of information received during the day and its retention in long-term memory occurs during sleep. Experiments confirm that during sleep, complex motor skills are also stored, not only learned information. Good-quality sleep is a prerequisite for effective education and training in all professions.

To sleep more deeply, and to be able to relax, do not overload the brain before bedtime. Read a book or take a walk. Do not work on the computer or watch TV, because these activities can irritate the nervous system so that sleep is superficial and does not provide complete relaxation.

Often, intelligence officers do not have enough time for sleep. This can cause sudden drowsiness, and there is a special method that can be used in such cases. Get comfortable and take a 20-minute nap, but not longer. Immediately after falling asleep, the brain goes into a stage of light sleep, which can be clearly seen on an encephalogram as high-amplitude theta waves. In this stage of sleep, it's very easy to wake someone up. About 20 minutes after falling asleep, a deep sleep with a predominance of slow delta waves sets in. A person who is woken up in a slow-wave sleep stage then feels sluggish and frustrated. Set the alarm for 20 minutes, or ask someone to wake you up. In most cases, such a short sleep will be enough to remove fatigue and enable you to complete urgent work. After waking up, have a cup of strong tea.

Exercise

Observe yourself for one or two weeks. Evaluate your performance on a seven-point scale ranging from -3 to +3, and record the data several times a day, making a graph. Summarizing this, you will get a cycle of average daily performance. After that, experiment with your schedule, observing the changes in your well-being. Maybe you will establish a more productive schedule.

Create a schedule so that the most complex tasks will be performed at the peak of your performance cycle.

★ Train your brain – Matches. Level 4

The exercise with the matches is more difficult: now you are paying attention to the pattern of the matches and which way the match head is pointing. Memorize both their positions.

Studying to be an intelligence officer is difficult. But the Disciplinary Code of the Soviet Military states: 'The soldier must endure all the hardships and privations of military service steadfastly and courageously.'

How not to leave things 'for later'

The intelligence service is not just a job; it's a way of life with high requirements. In particular, there is no place for procrastination. An agent cannot watch the news, read a book or prepare a cup of coffee or tea instead of completing their work.

In order not to waste time, it is useful to master techniques of self-organization. Here are some of them.

1. Lay down a goal for the task. Specify it and say why you are doing it. Imagine the result. Is it useful for you?

2. Divide the work into tasks with easily trackable results. Do not make them large. It is better to perform two or three tasks. It is important to experience pleasure in completing work. Reward yourself for these victories. Explain to yourself what you have done for the day and what you have achieved.

3. Perform only one task at any given time.

4. Reduce the number of external stimuli. Turn off your phone. Do not watch TV while working. Experiments clearly show that the human voice is distracting and reduces productivity. Put on headphones. Pick music that helps you focus on the job or work in silence.

5. Turn off e-mail and social networking notifications and social media. If you do not control the flow of information, it controls you.

6. Before work, tidy your desk. Preparation psychologically attunes you to efficient work.

7. Set aside time for work and time for fun and relaxation. Do not mix them; if you fully dedicate yourself to the work, you will free up time for a good rest. Checking e-mail and surfing the internet is not restful, especially when you need to work.

8. If you find it difficult to get down to work, try the following technique. Try to work for 30 minutes without distraction. If during this time you do not get into the rhythm of the task at hand, take a break or work on something else for the next 15 minutes, then try to work for 30 minutes again. If you get caught up in your work, and most likely you will, allow yourself to work for longer.

Effort is required in order to focus and hold attention, but when you get caught up in something, it is easier to concentrate. Focal attention will be replaced with automatic attention.

9. Celebrate productive days and weeks. Give yourself presents for achievements. Allow yourself to buy a good book or to go to a restaurant at the end of a successful week. Positive emotions confirm results.

10. To overcome procrastination, learn to manage your attention using exercises from this book. The better you master the technique of managing attention, the easier it will be to work and the more pleasure you will get from resting.

Exercise

To train the ability to concentrate, try working in difficult, distracting conditions. Turn on the TV, open a window or go to a noisy place. Over time, complicate the task: turn on the TV and radio at the same time.

This is a difficult exercise and at first it will be tedious for you. Give yourself a break when you finish.

Flow

In the course of studying prominent personalities, American psychologist Mihaly Csikszentmihalyi discovered that while working, everyone enters the same psychological state of being fully absorbed by their work. Csikszentmihalyi called this state 'flow'.

Someone in a flow state:

- has a clear understanding of the purpose of their work;

- is focused on their task, is not distracted by outside thoughts;

- loses self-awareness, self-evaluation is turned off;

- has a distorted sense of time: sometimes it goes by quickly and unnoticeably, sometimes it stretches out and allows you to complete more than expected;

- receives feedback quickly: results are immediately visible and the course of work can be quickly adjusted;

- feels a balance between skill level and the challenge presented: their work is not so easy that it is boring, but not so difficult that it is impossible to complete;

- feels personally in control of the situation and the outcome;

- enjoys the process of working and does not need to force themselves to perform their task.

Although everyone finds their flow differently, there are some general guidelines:

- set a goal;

- concentrate on the task;

- get feedback: keep track of the criteria of success, acknowledge your progress towards solving the problem;

- if the task seems boring, try to complicate it or to do better than last time;

- if the task is too difficult, improve your skills.

There is no space for procrastination if there is flow. Observe yourself, pick up techniques that help you to find your flow state.

Exercise

Think of a few cases where you have been in a state of flow. What were you doing? Who was with you? Where were you working? What was around you? How did you start working? What happened next? How did you feel? What do the times you entered your flow have in common?

Try to reconstruct these conditions and see if you can get into your flow state.

One thing at a time

When you're overwhelmed with work and do not have time to do everything you have scheduled for the day, there is a temptation to do more than one thing at a time, especially when you have forced pauses in some tasks.

For example, you need to draw up a report and check your e-mail. Isn't it logical to switch to e-mail when thinking about a difficult paragraph in the report?

But do not try to do two things at once. You might save a bit of time, but you will likely make a mistake in the report or miss an important message. In addition, you will get tired more quickly.

Initial concentration requires significant effort. Once you submerge yourself in work, it's much easier to maintain attention, which saves significant effort.

To understand how much effort it takes to shift attention, conduct a short experiment. Read the statements below. Evaluate the truth of every statement and remember the first word of each of them.

```
Dogs can swim.

Frogs do not have a moustache.

Elbows are the knees of arms.

Trains carry passengers.

Elephants do not eat meat.

Fish live in the air.

Frogs cannot breathe underwater.
```

Repeat the first words without looking at the statements. The correct answer is: dogs, frogs, elbows, trains, elephants, fish, frogs. It was difficult to remember them, wasn't it? This is because the task of checking the truth interfered with memorizing words.

Moreover, switching between tasks wastes energy, it does not allow you to enter into a flow state and enjoy your work.

★ Train your brain – Letter Pairs, 8×6

Now pick 24 pairs of letters and arrange them in a square 8x6. Train your working memory, trying to find matching pairs of letters. If it is still difficult for you to remember a large number of tiles, break it down into smaller pieces. For example, look for pairs of no more than eight different letters at a time.

1 August 1955

I've been in Moscow for nearly a week, and I'm still not over my trip to Argentina. So many experiences, a foreign language, a lot of work, different time zones. I sleep half the day and then don't sleep half the night. My head isn't working too well because of it. I feel like picking a fight or something all the time.

A lot of work has piled up in the almost-month I was gone. I'm trying to get through the pile evenly, without overtaxing myself. I've moved the most important things to my peak performance time — right now, that's only a couple of hours, from 9 to 11. I'm trying to find opportunities to sleep 15—20 minutes at a time during the day. I've added some physical stress to my routine — I run in the mornings and go to the pool. This lets me stay awake better and fall asleep faster.

5 August 1955,
Moscow

From the case file of operating investigation
of Argentine citizen Jose Alvarez
(Case #283)

According to agent information, Jose Alvarez has already
been of interest to the Second Main Directorate. He has
been put under surveillance on separate occasions, all of
which resulted in the conclusion that further interest in
Alvarez was unnecessary.

Alvarez has also come to the attention of the police. In
particular, the Moscow Criminal Investigation Department
suspected him of selling art objects illegally, but these
suspicions were not confirmed.

Alvarez's file contains photos operatives have taken of
Alvarez in the course of surveillance. During the photo
registration procedure, police noticed a resemblance
between Alvarez and the wanted Nazi criminal Erich
Finke. However, CID officers have not taken any actions in
response, as they have not had the opportunity to verify
the similarities.

According to available data, Alvarez is scheduled to
arrive in Moscow in October 1955 for an exhibition of
Latin American artists.

Activities: Upon arrival, establish surveillance (object
'Kind Soul'). When possible, perform an undercover
examination of his belongings.

Chief Operating Officer
of the Second Main Directorate
Major I. O. Miloslavsky

Stress and memory

Stress is an intelligence officer's constant companion. Contrary to popular belief, it is not entirely bad. At just the right time, the body can fall into a heightened state – the senses are tuned, the brain thinks clearly and the body is ready to act. Stress increases mental and physical abilities. However, when it accumulates, it can destroy a person. Prolonged stress without periods of recovery exhausts any organism. Fatigue interferes with work and perception becomes inadequate. Exhausted agents either exaggerate the danger of a situation or underestimate it, making mistakes in either scenario.

Prolonged stress has a negative impact on memory. Experiments on animals indicate that adverse conditions can lead to a decrease in the size of the hippocampus (the structure located in the medial temporal lobe of the brain that is responsible for long-term memory). Studies also confirm that people dealing with prolonged stress will have trouble with memorization and recall, as well as problems with memory interference.

Most methods of post-stress recovery are based on relaxation techniques: autogenic training, meditation, yoga, stretching, etc. All these techniques are well documented in literature. However, the most effective method for managing chronic stress is prevention. Rest regularly, let go of problems you do not have to solve and stop being a perfectionist.

★ Train your brain – Word dictation. Level 4

An intelligence officer often has no second chance to see a document, so he or she needs to remember everything the first time. Increase the number of words you are memorizing, using the loci or story method.

23 August 1955

Berlin.

Going through RSHA archives that our East German
colleagues have got hold of. Trying to figure out what
sort of experiments the Germans were doing. It makes
me sick. Went to Ravensbrück and Sachsenhausen
with them. Didn't help the case, but I had to see it
with my own eyes.

Trying to find Dachau survivors. Maybe they'll help me
find new threads tying Bernstein, Kovalev, Alvarez and
the missing documents together.

Berlin seems alive and joyful, although you can still
see traces of the war in some places. But even the
ruins and piles of rubble breathe German orderliness
and pedantry. I was advised to abstain from visiting
West Berlin.

- -

Re: Case #283
3 September 1955
Source: 'Simonides'
Received by: Major I. O. Miloslavsky

- -

On the past of Erich Finke

While in Berlin, under cover of researching the history of
psychology in West Germany for a journal article, gained
access to the RSHA archives in the Ministry of State
Security of the GDR. In addition, had a number of meetings
with former prisoners of concentration camps at Dachau,
living now in Karl-Marx-Stadt, Gorlitz, Frankfurt-an-der-
Oder.

Showed them pictures of Sigmund Rascher, Ernst Holtslehner
and Edward Vaiter, among others. Photographs of Jose
Alvarez were also among the pictures. Former prisoners
identified Rascher, Holtslehner and Vaiter as having served
in Dachau. They all noted the resemblance between Alvarez
and Erich Finke, who also served there. However, no one
confirmed that it is definitely him in the pictures.

Finke is remembered as a physician who worked in the group
of 'killer doctor' Sigmund Rascher. This team conducted
experiments on human beings in the Dachau concentration
camp.

Those questioned also indicated that Erich Finke and Ernst
Holtslehner also did experiments on super-cooling humans by
order of Hermann Göring. Prisoners were dressed in Luftwaffe
uniforms and placed into ice water, after which they were
warmed by various methods. These experiments were at once a
test of pilot uniforms and a way to find the best methods to
reanimate a person after severe hypothermia.

According to archival materials, hundreds of people
underwent experiments on hypothermia. All survivors were
subsequently destroyed by order of Rascher.

Berlin
#560

CONFIDENTIAL

Age and memory

Unfortunately, memory deteriorates with age. You can slow down the process through proper nutrition, exercise and work–rest balance, but it cannot be stopped. This is true for 'pure' memory – memory as a psycho-physiological function. However, practical memory does not deteriorate with age and may actually become stronger (if there are no medical problems).

The ability to remember depends on the richness of associations, which only increases with accumulated experience. With age, people develop practical techniques of processing in accordance with the complexity of the world. They keep a diary, record tasks and thoughts, learn how to work with large amounts of information, and can separate what is important from what is not.

Mnemonic methods are also good for keeping memory strong.

It might be helpful to an agent to know that in old age, people remember what they have learned in a lifetime, but do not recall the recent past as well. Professional skills remain intact for a long time, if not forever. There are many cases when people suffering from memory loss can do the work that they had been performing all of their lives. In this case, they are often unable to explain their actions and do not remember where and how they learned to do it. Professional habits help older people to maintain their identities, even if they left work many years ago. A retired military officer can be identified by his bearing and firm step.

Test yourself

Why did the Kolos restaurant waiter E. P.
Duzhkov remember Kovalev and Alvarez from 21
April 1955? (You may choose more than one
answer)

A) They gave a generous tip

B) They behaved unusually

C) The waiter said that one of the guests was a
   foreigner

D) The waiter had seen Kovalev before his lunch
   with Alvarez at Kolos

5
OPERATIVE

An operative is the workhorse of intelligence and counter-intelligence. They work in cooperation with agents and direct them, they interview people during the investigation and conduct external surveillance. They do detective work and are answerable for everything. Without them, intelligence is not possible.

Operative work is complex and the job requirements are often very high. He or she should be a good psychologist and be able to get on the right side of people. He or she should be highly intelligent, be able to compare data and synthesize information. He or she should have high working capacity and stress resistance. He or she should be able to keep secrets, because it's often vital not only for the success of the job, but also for the lives of his or her subordinate agents. And, of course, his or her memory should be sound.

Remembering faces and names

Intelligence officers should also learn to remember people. Not only their names and faces, but also their appearance, what they like, their hobbies, habits, weaknesses, past – everything that can help to establish contact in the future. Humans are social beings, so they have the genetic ability to recognize human faces, but need to work harder to remember names, favourite drinks, hobbies, etc. The best way to remember this information is to connect it to appearance.

Observe the person. Note his or her unusual features. This can be anything: a high or a low forehead, a unique nose or ear shape, wide- or close-set eyes, a dimple in his or her chin, a mole or a scar. Then, make up a story that connects the name to this feature. In order to better remember the story and the person, establish your emotional attitude. Do you like his or her main feature or not? Why?

When meeting someone for the first time, look at their face and listen to them. Visualize the unusual features of their appearance. If possible, talk to them, calling them by name. Try to repeat the name, recalling it from your visualization. Do not hesitate to ask again if you have forgotten it.

Exercise

Find unusual features in photographs of different people in newspapers or magazines. You should be able to process a face and identify its unusual features automatically.

Start with the face type that is common in your country. Then move on to faces from other continents.

7 September 1955,
Moscow

Because of the threat of discovery for agent 'Simonides',
I suggest a suspension of his work in the Philosophy
Department under the pretext of an extended leave of
absence to work on his thesis.

I request the enrolment of 'Simonides' in the staff of
the Second Main Directorate as an Operating Officer. His
background allows us to charge him with investigating
the case and communicating with agents in the Philosophy
Department of MSU.

                              Chief Operating Officer
                      of the Second Main Directorate
                              Major I. O. Miloslavsky

13 September 1955

Today, I signed my last time card. I no longer work at the university. I don't know yet what my new cover story will be.

After my trip to Berlin, I started getting looks at the university, people started whispering behind my back. On 2 September, when a huge party erupted in celebration of the beginning of classes, Kravchuk had too much vodka on an empty stomach and in his drunken frenzy poked me in the stomach, called me a snitch and talked about my trying to recruit him. Everyone giggled nervously and kept quiet.

I told my superiors about this and now I'm wondering whether being assigned to the office is a promotion or a punishment.

AGENT REPORT

- - - - - - - - - - - - - - - - -- - - - - - - - - - - - - - -

Re: Case #283
15 September 1955
Source: 'Michael'
Received by: Lieutenant Simonov

- - - - - - - - - - - - - - - - -- - - - - - - - - - - - - - -

On the last weeks of Kovalev's life
(transcribed from audiotape)

Kovalev's neighbour in the dorm informed me that shortly
before his death, he was reading a reprint of Leonid
Andreyev's story 'Judas Iscariot' and was very taken by
it.

The main idea of the book is Judas's moral distress.
In Andreyev's version, Judas betrayed Jesus and sent
him to his death only so that the prophets' prediction
could come true and his teachings wouldn't be forgotten.
For Andreyev, Judas became the person who allowed Jesus
to fulfil his destiny. Judas sacrificed himself and his
betrayal turned out for good.

Kovalev was deeply moved by this story, he was under its
sway for several weeks. Despite the fact that reading
Andreyev's story threatened Kovalev with expulsion from
university, he kept the reprint for a long time and spoke
to others about the story. The source reported that after
Kovalev retold the plot and the main idea of the story to
him, he spent a long time asking him what he would have
done if he had been Judas.

735

- -- - - - - - - - - - -

Note: tape is demagnetized

21 September 1955,
Moscow

From the case file of operating investigation
of Argentine citizen Jose Alvarez
(Case #283)

The following information has been received in response to
the request sent to the Ministry of State Security of the
GDR.

Erich Finke, b. 1905, doctor. Worked at the Luftwaffe
hospital. In 1942 with Sigmund Rascher and Ernst
Holtslehner, participated in criminal freezing experiments
in the concentration camp at Dachau.

Erich Finke's work focused on the application of
psychopharmacology (the use of psychotropic drugs),
hypnosis and manipulative techniques to large groups of
people.

Finke was also known to be fond of Italian Renaissance
painting. Had a fairly large collection of paintings,
which probably consisted of property confiscated from
prisoners. The collection was stored in his house in
Berlin. Often showed his pictures to colleagues and art
lovers. While working at the concentration camp sometimes
discussed art with the prisoners, which did not stop him
from conducting his experiments on them afterwards.

According to the documents, Erich Finke died in 1945 in a
military hospital in Neustadt (Holstein), five days before
Germany surrendered. However, there are reasons to suspect
that his certificate of death was falsified, and Finke fled
to Latin America. Finke's collection disappeared shortly
before Berlin was taken by Soviet troops.

Chief Operating Officer
of the Second Main Directorate
Major I. O. Miloslavsky

Memorizing information about people

When memorizing a name, you have been noting an unusual attribute, connecting it to the name and forming an emotional attitude towards it. Other information can be connected to the exaggerated attribute, not just a name. Preferences and interests can also help you find a common language.

For example, Mark Walker has a high forehead, likes chess, the TV show *House*, and gets annoyed when people watch football on television. Imagine this man with a high forehead painted like a chessboard. Imagine a little house in the middle of the chessboard, and a group of kids playing touch football in front of it. Suddenly, the ball goes flying right through the window and hits the television inside. An annoyed old man comes out of the little house pushing a walker in front of him. He writes on a piece of paper in red marker: 'NO FOOTBALL' and puts the sign on his door.

With practice, you will be able to create these pictures in a second or two and remember them for a long time.

Family is an important subject to everyone and one that you can use to make people trust you. It is important to remember family situations correctly so you do not accidentally, for example, ask a childless bachelor how his son is doing at school. You can also associate information about family with a main attribute too. Imagine an unusual story involving the family members vividly and emotionally.

Exercise

Continue studying the photos of people in magazines and newspapers. Study the appearance of interesting people, and remember information about them. This knowledge will be useful to you.

★ Train your brain – Profiles. Level 1

Remember the names and faces of people as you look through a newspaper. Notice unusual features in their appearances. Use vivid associations to link these with a name. Create an emotional attitude towards the person.

29 September 1955,
Moscow

<u>From the case file of operating investigation
of Argentine citizen Jose Alvarez</u>
(Case #283)

With the aim of further investigating Alvarez, a Soviet
agent residing in Paris met with French collectors and art
lovers. They confirmed that Alvarez had arranged private
painting exhibitions in Paris. They identified several
paintings from Alvarez's shows in a catalogue of objects
illegally exported by Germans from occupied territories
that had presumably belonged to Erich Finke.

Alvarez will arrive in Moscow on 11 October 1955.

Chief Operating Officer
of the Second Main Directorate
Major I. O. Miloslavsky

Verbal description

Protocols for describing someone's appearance, developed in the nineteenth century by the French criminologist Alphonse Bertillon, revolutionized the science of crime investigation. These techniques can help to identify a person, find them and confirm the presence of that person at a crime scene.

It is extremely useful to study how to compose verbal portraits. It helps to indicate what should be noticed when analysing appearance. In the future, this will allow you to remember someone better. A verbal portrait is then easily recounted to someone else, especially because it might be too risky to keep or transmit photos of the target. In this case, an accurate verbal portrait can secure the agent against a possible set-up, where an enemy counter-intelligence officer could make contact instead of the person you were supposed to meet.

The modern system of verbal description is based on four types of features:

- anatomical, describing the human body (sex, age, height, etc.);

- dynamic, apparent in motion (posture, facial expressions, etc.);

- distinctive, individual features (scars, missing body parts, a limp, etc.);

- additional features (clothing and how it is worn, accessories, etc.).

A verbal description is not just any description of the face and appearance, but a limited set of parameters for each feature. For example, the forehead in profile can be sloping, straight or protruding. Thus, a person is not so much described as typed. It radically simplifies the understanding of a verbal description given by someone else.

Here's a short version of a verbal description.

1. **Anatomical features**

A) Gender

B) Race, colour of the skin

C) Approximate age, with an accuracy of up to five years. For example, 20–25, 45–50

D) Height. For men: short (less than 5'6"), medium (5'6"–5'9"), tall (5'9"–6'2"), very tall (over 6'2"). For women these numbers are 2" less

E) Build: slight, average, full, stout

F) Hair
   – Colour: black, brown, dark brown, dark blond, light blond, red, grey
   – Texture: straight, wavy, curly
   – Beard, sideburns, moustache

G) Forehead
   – Height: high, medium, low
   – Profile: sloping, straight, protruding

H) Face shape
   – In front: round, oval, rectangular, trapezoidal, triangular
   – In profile: convex, straight, concave

I) Complexion (for Caucasians): pale, tan, red, yellow

J) Fullness of the face: thin, medium, full

K) Eyebrows
   – Colour: light, dark
   – Shape: straight, arched, twisting, joined
   – Form: tilted inwards, tilted outwards

L) Eyes
   – Location: deep-set, bulging
   – Colour: light, dark, grey, light blue, dark blue, green, brown, black

M) Nose
   – Length: small, medium, large
   – Width: thin, medium, wide
   – Shape: straight, concave, convex, wavy

N) Mouth
   – Size: small, medium, large
   – Corners of the mouth: horizontal, raised, drawn

O) Lips
   – Thickness: thin, medium, thick
   – Position of the upper lip relative to lower: upper protruding, lower protruding, even

P) Ears
   – Size: small, medium, large
   – Adherence: sticking out, close to head

2. **Dynamic features**

A) Step: fast, slow, waddling, bouncing, wobbly, shuffling. Limp, use of a cane or crutches

B) Posture: the slope of the head and neck forward (stooping), vertically (straight back)

C) Manners (unique actions): hands in the pockets, arms at sides, behind back, rubbing the hands. Smoothing the moustache, beard, or rubbing the forehead. Biting nails, spitting, holding a cigarette in a certain way

3. Distinctive features

Scars, birthmarks, baldness, hirsuteness, tattoos, facial or body asymmetry, body and other unique attributes

4. Additional features

Clothing, accessories: Particular attention is paid to the preference for any individual style, colour, fabric

Exercise

Continue working with photos of people. Make up their verbal descriptions using the system outlined on the preceding pages. Do this while watching movies, the news, and observing other people. An intelligence officer's observational skill consists of two things: knowledge of features worth noting and a lot of practice.

Exercise

Complicate the previous task. Try to describe a mutual friend, a famous actor or a politician to another person, so that they recognize him or her from your verbal description. Use the system described above when constructing the portrait. Then switch roles.

2 October 1955

I'm spending entire days preparing for Alvarez's arrival
and my meeting with him. I don't want to jinx it, but I
think the moment of truth is approaching. I just have
to make sure not to spook the Argentinian.

The various courses of our conversation branch and
sharpen every day. There must not be any surprises.
We're combing Moscow for an appropriate place to meet.
One place has too many people, another place is too
quiet, a third is inconvenient for external surveillance.

If Alvarez really did kill Kovalev, I have to be especially
careful. I really don't like the possibility of being
poisoned, even though our medics assure me that they
won't let me die. 'Too much honour,' they joke.

I'm most afraid of a dead end. What if nothing
works?

★ Train your brain – Profiles. Level 2

In this exercise, in addition to the face and name of each person, you need to remember their date of birth and occupation. Remember everything you can as you will need to recall the information in the final stage of the book.Birthday greetings are a good excuse for maintaining or renewing contact with a person you are interested in.

In addition to the exercise in this book, memorize the people you come across in your life. You never know where and when you may need such contacts.

Name: Alexei Popov
Date of Birth: 17/03/1971
Occupation: Diplomat

Name: Dina Petrov
Date of Birth: 03/12/1978
Occupation: Cleaner

Name: Vasilisa Sokolov
Date of Birth: 12/07/1977
Occupation: Waitress

Name: Vlad Mikhailov
Date of Birth: 14/05/1969
Occupation: Police Officer

Name: Inga Ivanov
Date of Birth: 01/11/1985
Occupation: Secretary

Name: Maxim Kuznetsov
Date of Birth: 11/02/1982
Occupation: Factory Worker

Test Yourself

What number appears under the memo headed
'On the last weeks of Kovalev's life'?

A) 247

B) 346

C) 479

D) 125

E) 925

★ Train your brain – Items on a table. Level 3

Memorizing the positions of items trains your memory and attention, develops
your observation skills, organizes your thinking. Try to also do this exercise in
your real life, remembering how books are placed on a shelf, how the things are
arranged on your desk, how cars are parked, etc.

Establishing contact

An intelligence service depends on its agents. Agents, ordinary people with access to information, can be recruited in different ways: some are offered money, some are blackmailed, others want to help for ideological reasons. But there is one thing that remains the same in working with any agent: recruitment and contact depend on communication. People want to be able to talk to someone and they are constantly in need of attention and support. Even when agents are coerced into working, the goal of a supervisor is to establish trust.

Typically, a potential agent is under a lot of stress during the first meeting. Not knowing what to expect from a recruiter, they see danger everywhere. One of the most important things to do is to give the agent confidence, relieve anxiety and tension. To do this, engage the agent in a non-threatening conversation, a conversation on safe ground.

A very good subject for conversation can be an agent's hobby. Everyone has something they can talk about endlessly. The hobby can be ordinary: stamps, chess, photography, football, or rare: growing cacti or oriental calligraphy. If you happen to find the hobby of your agent, talk less and just listen. You won't have to worry about starting a conversation, only finishing it.

If you do not know an agent's hobby, try guessing something important to them. Try to start with their profession. You can talk to an engineer about cars and machinery or to a teacher about today's students. People love to talk about themselves. Listen carefully, keep up the conversation, and you will find the right topic.

When trying to build trust, do not be afraid to discuss unfamiliar topics. Own up to your ignorance, ask and listen. Be genuinely interested. If your questions are not sincere, you will feel awkward, and your target will notice immediately.

Safe conversations relieve anxiety, create a sense of security and can identify the strengths of your conversation partner. For example, a gardener is patient, calm and kind, an engineer is clever, a teacher likes children. Emphasize these traits. Make it clear that they can be proud of them. Say that you do not have such merits. You are different, and acknowledge the superiority of your target. They will feel good about themselves and slightly embarrassed for a while, there will be a pause and you will be able to get to the main topic of the meeting.

Exercise

There are a lot of formal, superficial communications in life, such as with taxi drivers, postal workers, shop assistants, hairdressers, security guards. Use every such meeting as an opportunity to train yourself to establish trust. Talk to the person and try to guess his or her interests. Start a conversation with a taxi driver, asking, for example, about his/her experiences. Ask your hairdresser how s/he learned to cut hair. Praise goods in a shop. An unusual item in the workplace can also be a good opportunity for a dialogue. Experiment, pick different options for starting a conversation. Do not forget to give in, admitting that you do not have the skills and abilities of the other person.

You have nothing to lose if nothing comes of the conversation, but you will gain invaluable experience and, if successful, will learn a lot of interesting things.

SURVEILLANCE RESULTS FOR 'KIND SOUL'

12 October 1955,
Moscow

On 11 October, the target arrived in Moscow and settled into the Metropol hotel.

On 12 October at 11:15 he went to the Tretyakov Gallery, where he stayed until 14:20 under the surveillance of Seventh Main Directorate employees who were in the gallery as museum attendants. The object spoke to visitors several times to discuss the pictures. No items were delivered or received.

During this time, the object's room at the Metropol was searched. Nothing related to intelligence activities was found during the search. However, 'flags' that could be displaced during an unskilful search were discovered in the closet door, on the underwear and on the hanging suits: a piece of a match, a button from a shirt and the corner of a newspaper. All 'flags' found were returned to their places.

In the object's closet, 11 unprocessed rolls of 35mm colour film of foreign production were found. One roll was seized. In order not to arouse suspicion, a similar exposed film was left in its place.

The roll seized has been processed by a laboratory. The pictures on it were taken during a celebratory dinner. V. V. Romanov, a psychology instructor in the Philosophy Department of MSU, S. Y. Bernstein, an archivist of the Archives of the USSR, and V. M. Kovalev, a graduate student at MSU were identified in the photographs. The other people in the photos are currently being identified.

Chief Operating Officer
of the Seventh Main Directorate
Senior Lieutenant V. M. Nikiforov

124b

★ Train your brain – Items on a table. Level 4

If you have not already, increase the number of items to five. To memorize their locations, you may need a technique. Try to visualize how the objects would fall from a tilted table, how they would lie on the floor. If this method does not suit you, make up and use your own. Experiment, explore the individual attributes of your memory.

Notes

13 October 1955,
Moscow

From the case file of operating investigation
of Argentine citizen Jose Alvarez
(Case #283)

Subsequent to our discussion at the Congress of
Psychologists in Buenos Aires, Jose Alvarez proposed we
meet to discuss plans for collaboration. At the meeting,
Alvarez said that he was writing a book on art theory and
needed material on the history of experimental psychology
in Nazi Germany for one of the chapters. Alvarez said he
wanted to consult a professional psychologist, for which
he was willing to pay. He said he had already received an
advance from a US publisher.

When discussing my report, we spoke about archival sources
and the possibility of getting access to them. I showed
him copies of several documents from the RSHA Archives.
Alvarez was thrilled to see them. He also said that in the
course of collecting material for his book, he obtained
certain documents that could be of interest to me and
useful for my thesis. He was kind enough to agree to show
them to me if I could help him with his book.

At the end he asked me to keep the conversation a secret,
promising to do the same for his part.

Operating Officer
of the Ninth Division
of the Second Main Directorate
Lieutenant A. N. Simonov

Cover story

A cover story is a spy's claimed background or biography, which allows him or her to carry out a job.

A cover story provides a legitimate and reasonable justification for intelligence activities. Most intelligence officers are formal employees of embassies in a foreign country. They have diplomatic immunity and can't be prosecuted if they are exposed. In addition, many of them may be found on official business with different people, which means they can work with their agents almost openly.

Agents prefer professions that involve a wide range of communication: a journalist, a businessman, a teacher, a scientist, an art critic or a collector. This profession provides them with a basis for contacts with influential people, and in case of being exposed, makes it harder to prove involvement in espionage.

A cover story is thought out carefully and prepared before sending an intelligence officer on a mission. The cover story is compiled so that it is plausible, but does not look artificial. False information is mixed with genuine – fictionalized facts that have serious grounds. It's supported with documents and memorized details about the supposed place of origin of the agent, his or her studies and career, which are evidenced by registration entries made in archives and registries. Reasons for moves and switching jobs are thought out. The secret of a good cover story is that facts are difficult to check, and made-up information does not contradict the truth.

Sometimes a second cover story is created in case the first is uncovered, the purpose of which is to mitigate the consequences and take the heat off the officer's agents.

Cover stories are usually prepared by people who are not directly involved in intelligence operations. The task of an intelligence officer is to remember a cover story correctly, get into the role and to be able to reproduce it accurately if necessary. It is not always easy.

A cover story is extensive. It has a lot of important details and trivia. There was once a case when a Soviet agent deep undercover was asked about a scuff on the stairs of his previous house. The answer was checked and turned out to have been accurate.

An experienced intelligence officer may have several cover stories to juggle. They are easy to confuse under stress, especially the specific details.

Counter-intelligence also has its own ways of checking cover stories. For example, ask the person to repeat it in reverse order, from the present to the past. Reword the question, expand it or, conversely, make it more specific. Ask about details, and then compare the answers with information from other sources. If there are a lot of inconsistencies and contradictions or there are none at all, this is a reason for doubts.

Exercise

Retrace the last six months or year of your life in your mind. Remember all the events that occurred in that time with as many details as possible and make up a coherent story from your memories. Use all available materials: documents from a home archive, letters, bills and local newspapers. Ask family, friends and colleagues to supply extra information.

CONFIDENTIAL

15 October 1955,
Moscow

From the case file of operating investigation
of Argentine citizen Jose Alvarez
(Case #283)

On 15 October 1955 at 13:36 Jose Alvarez was arrested in
the lobby of the Metropol hotel during a meeting with
the operating officer 'Simonides'. When he was detained,
Alvarez was carrying photographic copies of experiments
done in the concentration camp at Dachau (in German, 17
sheets, 15x20 cm). Part of the stamp of the Archives of
the Academy of Sciences of the USSR is visible on one of
the pages.

Alvarez's room was searched. His suitcase was found to
have a secret compartment in which 15 processed black-and-
white 35mm films were discovered. Preliminary examination
shows that they contained copies of documents with Nazi
symbols.

Alvarez insists that he had nothing to do with the films
and is seeing them for the first time. He claims that he
only took photos of works of art, Moscow landscapes and
his friends.

Chief Operating Officer
of the Ninth Division
of the Second Main Directorate
Major I. O. Miloslavsky

15 October 1955

Wonderful news! Alvarez bit and got caught! He was arrested red-handed. He didn't even have time to put the photocopies down. I was very happy, but tried not to show it. Everyone who participated in the arrest was older and more experienced than I am — everyone worked so well and reliably — it was like they were reciting from memory.

Even though Alvarez put on a brave face during the arrest and kept calm, when he was searched, when they found the film, he visibly lost hope and started worrying. I think that was when I first smelled the scent of fear coming off another person.

And it is the smell of victory! How sweet it is!

★ Train your brain – Map. Level 3

Create a route on an unfamiliar map that is now longer and more complicated. Imagine the way the street you are mentally walking along looks. Make note of the turns. How does the way the street looks change? What can you see? Make your mental journey bright and unusual. Add some vivid and fantastic details.

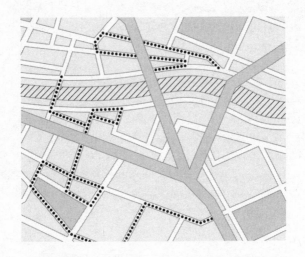

Memory for odours

For all living creatures, odour is a source of vital information. The sense of smell is a warning system, alerting us to danger signals, pointing to the proximity of food or another individual. For some species, smell is a means of communication. As humans evolved, our sense of smell got worse, but its influence is still significant.

Human olfactory memory is much stronger than visual or aural memory. Perhaps this is due to the strong neural connections between the area of the brain that receives signals from the olfactory receptors and the hippocampus, which is responsible for long-term memory. Odours are able to revive long-forgotten memories and the feelings associated with them. For example, the smell of home is remembered forever and recognized at once, bringing back the joys and frustrations of childhood. The perfume of a beloved woman can stir a man's emotions many years after separation, arousing seemingly extinct feelings.

Psychologists working with people who suffer from amnesia know that in some cases, important familiar odours can help to restore memory of events. Hypnotists also mentally 'place' people into a forgotten situation by helping them to focus on the odours associated with it.

You can also use the relationship between memory and the sense of smell. To immerse yourself in a situation that you or your informant want to remember, start with the odours.

Sometimes, smell can enhance memorization. If you want to remember a dinner conversation better, pay attention to the flavour of the food. This flavour, restored from memory, will give an additional association, which will help you to recall the dialogue.

Exercise

When you smell something familiar, try to remember where and when you smelled it before. What were you feeling? What were you doing? Who was with you?

Test yourself

What are the circumstances that made it reasonable to assume that Kovalev was involved in Bernstein's disappearance? (You may choose more than one answer)

A) Bernstein's friendship with Kovalev

B) Kovalev's avoidance of visiting places associated with Bernstein

C) Kovalev's sudden concern about the issues of moral evaluation of betrayal

D) The change of Kovalev's dissertation topic

6
ANALYST

Unlike agents and operatives, analysts are rarely shown in movies. But that does not mean that the analyst's job is not important. An analyst is a strategist. All the information collected by agents and operatives eventually trickles to them. They plan operations, they summarize intelligence information and present it to senior state leaders.

The work of an analyst is almost never dangerous and always very interesting. It is similar to the work of a detective. It is their job to recreate what was going on and determine the causes and effects of events based on scattered and contradictory scraps of information. They even decode foreign intelligence networks from isolated clues.

The highest class of analytical work is a sophisticated operative game, misleading enemy intelligence services through double agents, passing the truth off as a lie, a lie as the truth, and confusing opponents to gain an advantage.

An experienced analyst can determine the secrets of another state without leaving his office, using public sources – articles and reports, rumours and slips. Public sources provide 70% of intelligence information, and only a third of it is produced through secret operative work.

17 October 1955,
Moscow

<u>On the investigation into</u>
<u>missing documents containing classified information</u>
(Case #283)

Analysis of the documents of the RSHA, copies of which are
on Jose Alvarez's films, showed the following.

The documents contain research results from the Göring
Institute, including Erich Finke's reports and notes.
Finke himself appears in several of the photographs
illustrating experiment protocols. Pictures were taken
from multiple angles and are of high quality. From these
photos it is clear that Finke and Alvarez are the same
person.

Kovalev's notes indicate that he was familiar with the
contents of the RSHA documents that have been found,
and that he tried to use them for his thesis. Kovalev
probably began to suspect that Alvarez and Finke are
the same person, and that Alvarez/Finke was connected to
Bernstein's disappearance. Concerned about Kovalev's off-
balance state after the KGB interrogation, Alvarez may
have killed Kovalev as a dangerous witness.

Operating Officer
of the Ninth Division
of the Second Main Directorate
Lieutenant A. N. Simonov

★ Train your brain – Map. Level 4

Create your longest and most complicated route. Your task remains the same: retrace the route based on the location of buildings, canals and ponds, parks and gardens.

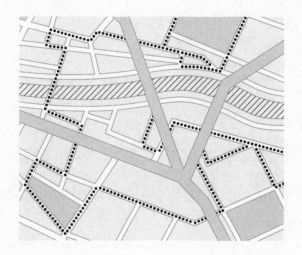

Prospective memory

Prospective memory is the ability to remember intentions or planned actions. Unlike retrospective memory, which is remembering events that really happened in the past, prospective memory has to deal with the future – something that is only intended and has not happened yet.

The act of remembering the future is initiated differently as there is no associated experience or past memory to be recalled. There is no such cue when it comes to our future intentions and recall is initiated by the person themselves.

The key difference can be explained with an example:

Retrospective memory: a wife asks her husband if he has bought bread. It's easy for the husband to reproduce the last two hours in memory and recall whether or not he has gone to the bakery. An external event indicates the need for recall – the wife's question. The husband does not need to think about this at a specific moment.

Prospective memory: a wife asks her husband to buy bread in the evening. There is no one to remind him to buy bread when he is going home from work. Most likely, he will not forget the request, but due to lack of external motivation, he risks not remembering it until he comes home. In other words, prospective memory consists of two parts: the memory of the intention and recall of the intention at the right time.

Prospective memory is very thoroughly studied by engineering, aviation and military psychologists. Most accidents and disasters are caused by humans making prospective memory errors: the operator forgets to do something, and it causes a chain of events with negative consequences. Air crash investigations show that pilots and air traffic controllers make most of their critical errors when they switch attention. For example, during a landing, a crew found that the downlock indicator on the dashboard was off. The pilot had had to make sure that the landing gear was down, but did this badly. The blown light bulb (which is what it was later discovered to be) diverted the attention of the crew, and the plane crashed into the ground.

In aviation, there are a lot of rules that compensate for prospective memory mistakes. These rules organize crucial actions so that they are minimally dependent on the attention and memory of a single person. For example, the stages of aircraft control are regulated by printed checklists and involve at least two crew members: one first performs an operation and reports on his or her actions aloud to the second, who checks the performance. There is a memorized, habitual and unquestioningly performed procedure for any manoeuvre. And yet, despite these measures, pilots sometimes make mistakes.

Prospective memory failures are very expensive for the intelligence service. A courier who forgets to wait for a countersign to his password jeopardizes his entire agent network. To prevent this, some methods that have long been used in aviation are used in the intelligence service.

★ Train your brain – Items on a table. Level 5

The task has become more complicated: place six objects on a table. Indicate their locations.

Prospective memory training

To determine how good your prospective memory is, answer the following questions:

- Do you forget birthdays, holidays and anniversaries?

- Do you forget to make tea after boiling water?

- Do you forget small requests and assignments and don't fulfil them?

- Do you go into a room, get distracted and forget why you went in?

- Do you sometimes lose your train of thought if you're interrupted in the middle of a conversation?

- Do you often forget what you wanted to take with you when you're leaving the house?

- Do you miss meetings with people because of your forgetfulness?

As already mentioned, prospective memory consists of two parts: the memory of the intention and the recall of it at the right time. There are many methods for training prospective memory, and you have already made a step forward by memorizing lists of words. But most mistakes in prospective memory occur in the second part, due to lack of external reminders.

If you want to improve your prospective memory, use the training method offered by American physiologist Stephen LaBerge. Set 'targets' – events that happen to you several times a day. For example, the target may be 'I see a 7', 'somebody is sweeping the street' or 'a woman in red is crossing the street'. Your goal will be to notice as many sevens, street cleaners or women in red as you can during the day. Consider how many times you have hit your target, and mark these events in your diary. Analyse the statistics of the hits per week. Train with one target for a few days, and then choose another one. Start with one target, then work simultaneously with two or three. This will strenghten the relationshop between the two parts of your prospective memory.

Exercise

Training with target events will develop your ability to remember intentions in response to an external event. However, this is not enough for good prospective memory: you must be able to remember your intention at the right time. An intelligence officer, more than anyone else, is expected to have a great sense of time. First, it will help you recall what you need at the right time without external prompts. Second, you will be able to plan your obligations more precisely, being clearly aware of how long it takes to do your work.

When constantly relying on a clock, modern humans do not use their internal sense of time, and it is gradually lost. To get it back, you should rely on your intuition more often.

Exercise

Note the time on a stopwatch or a watch with a second hand. Not looking at the watch, try to say when a minute has passed. Five minutes. Ten. An hour. Do not count seconds, be engaged with what you are otherwise doing. If your inner clock is slow or in a hurry, check it and try again.

Exercise

Spend one day without a watch. It would be even better not to
use a cell phone that day. It will make you take a look at how
you spend your time.

Exercise

When starting a task, try to predict how long it will take. Do
not look at your watch while working. When the task is done,
compare the actual time it took with your forecast. How far
off was your prediction? Did you overestimate or underestimate?
Start with small and simple tasks: writing e-mail, cleaning a
room. Having achieved a certain precision, move on to larger
tasks and projects.

How to help prospective memory

Prospective memory is meant to store information about intentions and to remind you about them in time. This section describes practical techniques that can help you to remember things at the right time.

The easiest method of reminding yourself of anything is to change your environment and make it unusual, and therefore noticeable. For example, you can put your trainers near your toothbrush so as not to forget to do your morning exercises. An unusual way to remember that you have to take something with you is to leave your car keys in the refrigerator. Having found them in an unusual place, you will not forget to bring along a book that you promised to give to your colleague.

You can continually remind yourself of an important task, both at relevant and irrelevant times. A good example of this practice is to draw a cross on your hand. People see their hands almost constantly, and the cross will continually remind you that you need to complete an outstanding task.

Pocket planners and schedules support prospective memory. A to-do list is not just a list of tasks, it is a behavioural strategy. Remembering intentions is associated with the habit of checking your schedule before starting to work and at the end of each task. Thus, a person starts to work after external reminders, which supports the inner impulse of prospective memory.

Schedules can be used for planning tasks for more than one day. In order not to forget to contact relatives and friends during holidays, write the dates of anniversaries and birthdays in the calendar and make it a rule to check these for the week ahead every Monday. The same calendar can be used for regular medical examinations, pet vaccinations, utility payments, tax filing, etc. It will help you to do everything in time and not to forget the events that occur too rarely to always remember them. Of course, the schedule of anniversaries and birthdays can be electronic, with automatic reminders, but in this case, you are not involved in recall, and it weakens your prospective memory.

Another behavioural strategy is regularly 'scanning' your intentions. If you make it a rule to think about shopping every time you drive past the store, you will not forget to buy food.

Events and intentions can be linked directly or, on the contrary, in most peculiar ways. The first day of each month is a time to go through all of the bills you have received and to schedule payments of them. Good weather brings to mind thoughts of taking a vacation.

Test Yourself

What is the date noted on Andrei Simanov's first journal entry?

A) December 1954

B) January 1954

C) March 1956

D) June 1955

Exercise

Invent your own rules for scanning tasks that you want to do. Start with one or two. Select events in response to which you will scan your intentions: leaving the house, leaving the office, driving past the store, a pedestrian crossing the street, a specific time or date, a meeting with someone.

Follow these rules. Make them a habit. Gradually increase the number of rules in accordance with your goals and needs.

The mnemonic devices described earlier can also be used for prospective memory. Think of an event or an occasion for recalling a planned task. Imagine a bright emotional picture with the event and the task. For example, if you want to buy a collection of lectures by Sigmund Freud, an event for it can be 'driving past the bookstore'. Imagine that you are driving past your favourite bookstore and get into a traffic jam. Dr Freud himself has created this traffic jam. Smoking a cigar, he is signing books in the middle of the street, causing the traffic jam.

Finally, the most effective way not to forget things is to follow rules and rituals. There are a lot of such rules in the intelligence service. The art of secrecy follows a set of rules: what to do before, during and after meeting with an agent, what and how to talk about your work, how to answer tough questions and to evade surveillance. Any mistake can be fatal. In this way, the intelligence service is similar to aviation, and so it uses the same techniques that pilots use: regulations and checklists. The only difference is that an intelligence officer does not store documents, but remembers them.

As mentioned before, prospective memory mistakes occur mainly because of distractions during important procedures. To reduce the number of such mistakes, do not switch to another task after being distracted. Pause. Fix where you were in your memory. Create and mentally play a new plan in which you postpone your first task, then the second, and then return to the first one. Since the task is not competed there will be a mark in memory that will remind you to go back and finish it. Think about the Zeigarnik effect.

Exercise

Create rituals and checklists for tasks that you perform often. If you forget to take necessary things with you when leaving, write a list. Memorize it. When getting ready, recall each item and check whether it is already in your bag.

Checklists for repetitive actions will save you time and effort. Let your first checklist be for all the things you take with you when going to work.

Sometimes prospective memory can make very strange mistakes. A person may forget whether or not they have done something important: turning off the iron, locking the car or feeding the cat. This is because the action is carried out habitually, not quite consciously. The fact that it has been completed is not remembered, but the intention to do it remains. There is concern for possible consequences. If something like this happens to you often, set a target event like leaving the house or leaving the car. Connect this event with an action to make sure that all the electrical appliances are turned off. Make a mental note of completing the actions.

11 November 1955,
Moscow

On the investigation into missing documents
containing classified information

(Case #283)

Former Dachau prisoners Rudolf Adler, Carl Salmon and
Michael Livshits were invited from the GDR for a face-
to-face confrontation with Jose Alvarez. During the
confrontation, they clearly identified Jose Alvarez as
the German doctor Erich Finke. Identifiers noted not only
a visual resemblance, but similarity in gait, manner of
moving and facial mimicry.

Chief Operating Officer
of the Ninth Division
of the Second Main Directorate
Major I. O. Miloslavsky

6 February 1956,
Moscow

As a result of the investigation into missing documents
containing the classified results of psychological studies
in Nazi Germany from the Archive of the Academy of
Sciences, I can report the following.

During the investigation it was determined that Jose
Alvarez and war criminal Erich Finke are the same person.

There is also strong evidence of Alvarez spying against
the Soviet Union. There was no opportunity to determine
who he was working for, but we can assume that it was
a community of former Nazis who fled to Latin America
after the defeat of Fascism and were fostering hopes for
a resurgence of Nazi ideology. Perhaps Alvarez-Finke's
motive was concealing his crimes in Dachau, but in that
case it is not clear why he needed to make photographic
copies of documents.

There are reasons to believe that Alvarez-Finke is
connected with the disappearance of the Archives employee
S. Y. Bernstein. Bernstein carried documents out of
the Archives in violation of security regulations. He
allowed Kovalev to access them, which is how certain
ideas contained within found their way into the latter's
dissertation drafts.

Alvarez found out from Kovalev about the existence
of these documents, and that Bernstein had access to
them. Alvarez probably tried to take possession of the
documents, doing away with Bernstein to this end. Since
Bernstein's body was never found, Alvarez's involvement in
Bernstein's murder was never proven.

cont.

One can also assume that on 21 April Alvarez poisoned
Kovalev during the meeting at the Kolos restaurant.
Kovalev was a paid agent of Alvarez, probably without
knowing it, however he later realized that he was an
accessory to Bernstein's murder. Alvarez's involvement in
Kovalev's murder also cannot be proven, since the autopsy
of Kovalev's body did not show any known poisons.

The case was submitted to the court. Jose Alvarez is
charged with two counts: war crimes and espionage.

> Head of the Second Main Directorate
> KGB of the USSR
> Lieutenant General P. V. Fedotov

#15g

★ Train your brain – Matches. Level 5

Continue your practice, but increase the number of matches to fifteen.

The exercises are very difficult at the final levels. Do not give up if you do not succeed right away.

★ Train your brain – Word list. Level 7

When you master the skill of memorizing lists, the number of words on the list should be of no further consequence. It is important to learn how to memorize words as quickly as possible.

When training, alternate using the story method and the method of loci.

Working with information
in the intelligence service

Contrary to popular belief, the intelligence service is not just about securing information through illegal means. First, not all necessary information is confidential. Most of the information is gathered from public sources and by legitimate means: from the press, advertising materials, at conferences and exhibitions and in ordinary professional communication. Facts themselves, which can be conflicting, do not provide anything towards making important decisions. The most important task is the analysis of available data.

With this understanding of the intelligence service, data collection becomes an important auxiliary step in creating a reliable picture of a situation. You can collect primary data endlessly, but your report is due by a certain time. Basing decisions on a specific assignment and the availability of time, an analyst plans what data and what degree of reliability they need.

It is important to understand that data from different sources has various degrees of reliability. Usually, the intelligence officer balances between reliability and timeliness, and does not always prefer reliability. An analyst has to deal not only with the truth, but with probability.

What should you, an intelligence analyst, do, having received an assignment? First, estimate how much time you have. The timeliness of a task means a lot in the intelligence service. Information gets outdated quickly, and a full, verified report is almost too late.

Then familiarize yourself with the problem and define the boundaries of analysis. Identify primary and secondary data. Concentrate on what is important. Collecting all possible information without any plan can be too time-consuming and demanding.

Start collecting open-source material. Sometimes it will be repetitive. Different sources may conflict or disagree with each other. Do not worry. This could be caused by different methods of collecting and reporting information. Or the problem could lie in the reliability of your sources. Compare the data, evaluate it and find confirmation for it or refute it.

Analysis of indirect data can be infinitely useful. For example, the exact date of the launch of a manned spacecraft is strictly classified, and it is almost impossible to find it out directly. But, for example, and this has been practically tested, you know that food for astronauts is prepared within one or two weeks of their departure, so that it is fresh for a launch. Secrecy in food services is a much lower priority than in technical services. Monitoring the work of the food services associated with the spaceship, or of its workers' contacts, can help to determine the launch date to within a week.

Once you have worked through the available open-source material, go back to the original plan. Specify what important information is still unknown. Make a plan for further research. Assess your resources and, if appropriate, submit a request to headquarters for classified information.

In a broader sense, the goal of the intelligence service is to create a reliable picture of the present and to make forecasts for the future in any field of public interest: military, politics, economics, science or technology. The intelligence service is interested in three types of information about foreign states: the present state of affairs (what they do), capabilities (what they can do) and intentions (what they are going to do).

Exercise

Forecast how some problem concerning you will be resolved. Will a road be built through the park near your house? Which of your colleagues will be promoted to be head of the department? Can your favourite sports team get into the play-offs this season? Determine what forces affect the outcome, who of the players is interested and who has a greater impact on the final result. Collect open-source information and assess its credibility. Answer three questions: (1) What is the present situation? (2) What are the capabilities of all the participants? (3) What are their intentions? The future will show whether you were right.

★ Train your brain – Crossword 7x7

At this level, the size of the matrix has almost reached the size of a chessboard: 7x7 cells. Group the dark cells in shapes, letters or numbers. This way, you reduce the number of objects to memorize.

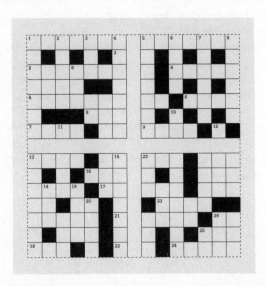

Facts and pictures

In an analyst's work, it is much more useful to compare facts than to analyse each fact separately. For example, the fact that the number of students from country X studying nuclear physics abroad has doubled, in itself doesn't add up to much. Perhaps the growth corresponds with a general trend of young professionals leaving the country.

But if we compare this fact with others, then we may see a different picture:

- a factory in a remote province of country X buys a powerful industrial centrifuge;

- a railroad leading to this factory is being equipped with a modern video surveillance system;

- the largest railway company in country X places an order for the construction of special trains for transportation of hazardous materials;

- construction of an additional pool for cooling fuel elements is begun at a nuclear energy station in country X.

All these facts allow us to formulate a reasonable hypothesis: the government of X is developing technology for processing and enriching spent nuclear fuel. Monitoring the railroad and records of trains arriving to the plant allows us to make quantitative conclusions about the extent and pace of construction.

Note that this hypothesis does not require undercover penetration into the nuclear energy organizations of country X. It is enough to simply monitor the state's commissions, to have a few conversations with seasonal construction workers and minor agents living near the railroad.

Sometimes an analyst needs to make a lot of observations. Comparing the most common data can lead to unexpected results. For example, this schedule shows the days counter-intelligence officer A, a forty-three-year-old man, works overtime: 2 March, 5 March, 6 March, 11 March, 15 March, 20 March, 21 March, 2 April, 4 April, 7 April, 11 April, 13 April, 20 April, 2 May, 15 May. By itself, it does not mean anything. Neither does the overtime schedule of officer B from another department, a twenty-eight-year-old woman: 27 February, 5 March, 7 March, 11 March, 15 March, 20 March, 2 April, 4 April, 6 April, 15 April, 24 April, 5 June. But when this information is compared:

A: 2.03, 5.03, 6.03, 11.03, 15.03, 20.03, 21.03,

2.04, 4.04, 7.04, 11.04, 13.04, 20.04, 2.05, 15.05.

B: 27.02, 5.03, 7.03, 11.03, 15.03, 20.03, 2.04,

4.04, 6.04, 15.04, 24.04, 5.06

We might guess that A has established a friendship with B, which either ended in early April, or moved on to another phase (and they meet outside of work). This is not a final conclusion, but an assumption, which is easy to verify.

Statistics give powerful data-mining tools to an intelligence officer. But they must be used carefully. Using statistical methods requires a sufficiently large amount of data, specialized training, and carefully formulated hypotheses that will be tested with the help of statistics. Injudicious use of statistics without reasonable justification of derived correlations can lead to useless or wrong conclusions: 'All people who eat cucumbers die, therefore cucumbers are deadly.'

Exercise

Estimate the weekly earnings of your favourite cafe. Explain the method you used. Come up with several ways to make this estimation. Use all available information: the number of seats and tables, the menu, information from the bill, other people's stories, your own observations and experiments.

Check your conclusions, making contact with someone from the staff: waiters are well aware of the earnings of a cafe, since their tips depend on it.

Crime and punishment –
the scientific method

The work of an analyst is similar to the work of a scientist or an investigator. They need to collect unrelated facts and build a coherent picture on their basis. A comparison of all known facts in the hope of finding any regularity would take too long and does not guarantee results. To make this process consistent, analysts use the research model adopted by modern science, including criminology.

Stage 1: Facts. Gather basic known facts about the subject. Try to imagine them visually, making a scheme or a mind map. If possible, study existing theories, opinions and points of view. Keep in mind that some data may not be completely accurate and reliable, and theories can be incomplete or erroneous. At this stage, an investigator examines the crime scene and interviews witnesses.

Stage 2: Hypothesis. Formulate a hypothesis (an assumption that explains the facts in the best way). During an investigation, an investigator suggests who committed the crime and how, on the basis of evidence and the testimony of witnesses. For example, the head of a large organization was shot. Crime scene investigation and interviews of colleagues allow us to hypothesize that the crime was committed by one of the subordinates of the victim and the motive could be the desire to take his job.

Stage 3: Conclusions. Think of what follows from your hypothesis and whether it is true. The consequences of the hypothesis must go beyond the limits of available facts, stating more than was known at first. Going on with the above example, the investigator may argue as follows. The body was found half an hour after the crime. According to the security guard, no staff left the office before the police arrived, therefore the instrument of the crime and the killer are still in the building.

Stage 4: Verification. Develop a hypothesis. Look for new facts that can confirm or refute conclusions drawn from the hypothesis you made in the previous stage. One way to obtain new facts is to conduct an experiment. If new facts refute your theory, exclude or modify the hypothesis and go back to stages 1 and 2. Formulate a new hypothesis based on additional facts. If you were able to confirm most of the consequences, the hypothesis can be conventionally considered proven. It is only conditionally proven, because some day you might find facts that refute it. Typically, scientists put more effort into disproving a hypothesis, whereas investigators, unfortunately, try to confirm it.

The hypothesis (murder by a subordinate) and the conclusion (the gun in the office) give a direction to further research. We know what to look for (a gun) and where (in the office). It's better than looking for an unknown object in an unknown place. Finding the gun allows us to develop the original hypothesis. If the gun is not found, an investigator should figure out how it was carried out of the office or formulate another hypothesis.

Using the earlier example of the development of technology for the processing of spent nuclear fuel, we can construct the following chain of reasoning.

Stage 1. Facts

1. The number of students studying nuclear physics has doubled;

2. A major chemical company has purchased a powerful centrifuge;

3. The railroad branch that goes to the factory is equipped with a video surveillance system;

4. A special train for transportation of hazardous materials has been ordered;

5. An extra pool for cooling spent fuel elements is being built in a major nuclear power plant.

Stage 2. Hypothesis

Government X is developing technology for processing and enriching spent nuclear fuel. The construction of an additional cooling pool speaks to the intention of accumulating spent fuel elements. Safety measures on the railroad can mean a change in the direction and volume of transportation of critical goods. An increasing number of specialists shows that a new policy in the field of nuclear energy is being implemented seriously and for the long term. It also speaks to the special nature of the proposed work; otherwise the country would invite foreign specialists.

Stage 3. Conclusions

If the hypothesis is true, then:

- radiation levels in the area of the chemical plant will increase;

- contaminated airbursts will appear;

- the company will buy nitric acid, which is necessary to dissolve solid radioactive waste;

- the engineering infrastructure of the plant will become more sophisticated: cementation, vitrification and bituminization, all used in the disposal of nuclear waste, are very complex production processes;

- an armoured train with special containers will operate regularly from the nuclear power plant to the factory.

In order to be able to draw these conclusions, you don't need to do any more than acquaint yourself with the technology used for processing nuclear waste, which can be done by using open sources, such as sites of international atomic agencies or conservation organizations.

Stage 4. Verification

Reports of increased radiation levels and emission of radioactive gases may appear in the mass media or on 'green' sites. It may be necessary to use a network of agents in country X to take water and air samples for chemical analysis and watch the movement of trains on the railroad.

If the conclusions and hypotheses are confirmed at the fourth stage, it is most likely that they are accurate, and then you need to act based on this. Otherwise you will need a new hypothesis as to what is going on.

Scientific research is a formal and creative procedure. It's formal because proof or disproof of the hypothesis is based on the laws of logic. It's creative because a hypothesis is born thanks to insight. Nevertheless, the scientific method saves a lot of time and resources. Information research becomes directional. We do not waste time on insignificant data extraction. As a result, decisions are made more quickly, reducing the risk for agents.

Using the scientific method, try to follow these well-tested guidelines:

1. Formulate a working hypothesis as soon as possible. Haphazard collection of facts delays the solution of the problem.

2. Treat the hypothesis critically. It's easy to be misled by fitting facts to a hypothesis.

3. Be ready to start all over again. Refutation of a hypothesis is not defeat, but a step towards the truth.

4. Creating a good hypothesis takes time. If you are at an impasse, take a break.

Decisions should have time to ripen.

Exercise

Try to learn more about people you do not usually pay attention to. For example, watch the receptionist at your work. Does she have a family? If she knits bright socks, we can assume that she has grandchildren. Test this hypothesis by talking to her. Try to give her something for her grandchildren, she will accept the gift or refuse it, explaining her decision.

Find out the work schedule of the security staff in your office. Try to guess and check where your greengrocer is from.

Exercise

Try to understand the politics of your country to a greater depth than most people. Try to figure out what is not said openly. Gather facts, compare, formulate hypotheses and generate forecasts. Time will tell you whether you were right.

Test yourself

What facts allowed investigators to establish
a connection between Bernstein and Alvarez?
(You may pick more than one answer)

A) The fact that Alvarez knew Kovalev,
a friend of Bernstein

B) Bernstein's presence in pictures taken by
Alvarez

C) The fact that Alvarez knew Bernstein,
discovered during his meeting with Simonides
in Buenos Aires

D) Operatives of Seventh Main Directorate of the
KGB finding documents from the Archives of
the RSHA during a search of Alvarez's hotel
room

E) Alvarez showing agent Simonides a photocopy
of RSHA documents during a meeting in Moscow

F) The discovery of photocopies of documents
missing from the Archives of the Academy of
Sciences of the USSR that Bernstein was
responsible for in Alvarez's room after his
arrest.

7
DOUBLE
AGENT

Sometimes an agent or operative is found out, or compromised, as the intelligence service calls it. Then the intelligence service that uncovered the agent might offer them a 'second job'. The compromised agent can agree and not report this to the intelligence service of their government. Or they can accept the job with the approval of their supervisors.

In the first case, the agent is a traitor. Sometimes it is advantageous, but it is always shameful. In the second case, they continue to serve their country under a different status, trying to mislead the new 'employer'.

If an ordinary agent leads a double life, the double agent lives a triple life. They cannot lose their self-control even for a moment, nothing can ever be confused or forgotten.

Displacement

Freud believed that the human psyche consists of the conscious and subconscious. Each of these are governed by their own laws. To illustrate this, Freud used the metaphor of the iceberg: an outside observer sees only the small surface area of a mass of ice, but 90% of it is hidden under water. Similarly, most of the human psyche is beyond consciousness and affects human feelings, thoughts and behaviour covertly.

Freud argued that there are forbidden desires, feelings and thoughts in the subconscious mind. The circumstances that cause them are often also displaced. Thus, by ignoring and forgetting, a person solves inner conflicts and reaches a comfortable existence. Psychotherapists confirm many cases of psychogenic amnesia when patients forget the circumstances of extreme situations they have experienced. In cases where the emotions of the incident become unbearable, people sink into oblivion.

Debates about Freud's theory have gone on for over a hundred years. Some psychologists accuse psychoanalysis of being unscientific and not having experimental confirmation. Others recognize its value and successfully use it in clinical practice.

According to Freud, the conflicts between consciousness and the displaced content of the subconscious mind can lead to mental disorders: anxiety, depression and obsessive-compulsive disorder. Freud proposed to treat such disorders with psychoanalysis (special conversation with the psychoanalyst to help the person understand the causes of internal conflict). Freud asserted that the retrieval of the causes of painful symptoms from the subconscious is enough to relieve tension and lead to healing.

Freud developed several methods of analysing the subconscious. One of them is the free association method: a person says whatever comes into her or his head. At some point, the monologue is interrupted, as if the person has bumped into an obstacle. This means that they have reached important information that has been displaced from the consciousness and have recalled it. Another method is dream interpretation. The characters and plot of a dream indicate the content of the subconscious. By interpreting a dream, an analyst helps to realize displaced feelings, desires and memories.

An important conclusion from Freud's displacement theory is that people tend to forget unpleasant things. People often erase actions that cause guilt and shame from their memories: crime, deceit, callousness. People forget small debts, requests, orders and unfulfilled promises. Sometimes things become partially modified in human memory. For example, a person remembers a situation, the actions and words of others, but does not remember what they did themselves.

An intelligence officer often has to deal with displaced memories following a traumatic event. To help a person to recall them, you can use psychoanalytic techniques. Suggest that an informant talks about everything that comes to mind when thinking about the event, even if it is not connected directly. Analyse the monologue. Note everything that may be associated with the event, directly or indirectly. Once a person pauses or stops, ask him or her to tell you what they were thinking about. Support the person, make clear that you will not blame him or her for anything they tell you. Go from one association to another. There is a high chance that some of the expressed thoughts will give you the information you want or allow the informant to recall something displaced.

Remember that the memory of traumatic situations (the deaths of loved ones, acts of terrorism, military actions) can be painful. When working with severe mental trauma, seek the assistance of a qualified psychologist.

Exercise

Keeping a diary of dreams is not only a fun path to self-knowledge, but also an effective form of training for the memory. To remember your dream, put a notebook and a pen next to your bed. Immediately after waking up, without getting out of bed, write down the plot of your dream in a few words. Pay attention to the feelings that you experienced in the dream. Then, no later than noon, review your notes and write down the dream in more detail. Some stories and images will be repeated, they will point out something important to you, something that you care a lot about.

Freud appreciated dream interpretation; he called dreams 'the royal road to the unconscious'. Dreams really have great value and help to solve many problems and challenges. Dreams have prompted the creation of important scientific ideas such as the ring structure of the benzene molecule and the periodic system of chemical elements.

★ Train your brain – Crossword 12×8

Mentally group the darkened cells. Arrange them in imaginary figures and shapes.

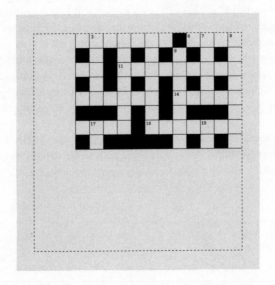

False memories

What is memory? Is it a database or a reconstruction process for data? Modern psychology says that it's a process. Memories of the past are reconstructed every time they are accessed. On the one hand, this means that forgotten information can be restored: using the fragments remaining in memory, we can recreate the whole picture. On the other hand, every new reconstruction changes memories.

French psychologist Jean Piaget describes a case from his life. He remembered in detail that when he was about two years old, someone tried to steal him out of his stroller. Piaget could describe the scene of the kidnapping, how his nurse tried to block him, and how the criminal ran away when he saw a policeman. He was confident in his memories until he was fifteen, when the nurse turned to religion and wrote to Jean's parents that she invented the whole story from beginning to end. The psychologist had probably heard this legend retold by his parents many times until he recreated it visually, and remembered it as a true event. This example shows that a person can be absolutely sure of the reliability of his or her memory while reproducing false events.

Childhood memories are often untrue. This is due to a phenomenon that psychologists call child amnesia, when a person forgets the first few years of his or her life. There are several theories on this subject: from psychoanalytic (which explains forgetting through displacement of child conflicts) to neurobiological (the immaturity of brain structures in early childhood). The most convincing is the current understanding of the development of long-term memory in conjunction with the development of abstract thinking and language. A child does not learn enough concepts in the first years of life to be able to fix what happens to him/her in his/her memory.

Nevertheless, many people remember faces, toys, episodes and events from early childhood. However, as a rule, these memories are formed on the basis of photographs and the stories of adults, as in the case of the Piaget abduction.

But do not think that false memories only fill gaps related to children's amnesia. They may appear due to mistakes of perception: people see what they want to see, ignore what contradicts their beliefs and complete the picture in accordance with these beliefs. A witness who believes that most crimes are committed by the homeless will describe a criminal as homeless. They may not notice the features of a wealthy citizen and will complement the description with other details. They will reconstruct the event based on his or her stereotypes, but will be sure that they remember everything exactly and accurately.

Another source of false memories is conformity. This is the act of matching attitudes, beliefs and behaviours to group social norms. Numerous psychological experiments have shown how easily people fall under the influence of a charismatic character or under the pressure of assistants playing the role of other subjects in an experiment. Some people are even ready to deny something obvious or confirm a lie if they see other subjects doing the same. More than 40% of test subjects recognized that a group of lines was the same length, even though it was obvious that the lines were different, because the group that performed before them did the same. Thus, the memories of people who easily fall under the influence of others may have been suggested to them, especially if they were originally set out by authoritative or powerful people and repeated many times.

False memories differ from outright lies. Reproducing them, a person is sincerely mistaken. They speak confidently, because they believe in their words. There is often an internal logic in their memories.

Intelligence officers who are constantly working with informants are often faced with false memories. Thus, they have to recheck data. The first way to separate the truth from falsehood is to compare information from different sources. When information from different people coincides, it's likely to be correct. If the information differs, you need to evaluate which source is more reliable. Another way to separate true memories is to ascertain consistently and thoroughly what the person really saw and heard, and what they thought throughout.

Test Yourself

In the 'Crime and Punishment' method section, what had a major company purchased?

A) A railroad

B) Video surveillance

C) Hazardous materials

D) A centrifuge

Exercise

A couple of days after an event (a celebration, a party or a picnic) ask everyone who was there about it. Who was present? Who was wearing what? Who was sitting where? What was the conversation about? What was on the table? Who came and went when? You will find some striking differences between the versions of different people. If possible, look at photos and videos of events and evaluate the reliability of memories.

Exercise

Explore the most vivid memories of your childhood. Compare them with stories of parents and relatives. Consider family photos of that time and saved video. If you find differences, try to figure out how they emerged.

Exercise

Develop an autobiography. Restore your life history from birth to the present time year by year. Remember where you lived, what you did, who you were friends with. Ask those who knew you, compare your memories with family photos and documents. Find old friends, classmates and course mates and contact former colleagues. It will be great practice for composing a convincing cover story for an intelligence officer.

Manipulation of memories

The fragility of memories can cast doubt on the testimonies and information provided by informants. Recollections can be false because of a mistake or because of a deliberate suggestion planted by another person.

Experienced lawyers know how to discredit eyewitness testimony. By asking complicated questions about details, they create doubt in the witness's mind, which allows them to conclude that the entire testimony is unreliable.

For example, when asked about the colour of a Citroën in which robbers sped up to a bank, a witness says 'green'. Under pressure from the lawyer, they remember the colour of the car. The witness did not see the car approaching the bank and couldn't identify the model. However, with the help of the lawyer's leading question, the witness reconstructs their memories and, most importantly, begins believing in them. Yes, it was a green Citroën, and it came to the bank at full speed. After hearing the testimony, the lawyer compares it with camera records, where an old green Ford slowly drags itself to the bank. The apparent discrepancies discredit the testimony of a witness in court and make him or her doubt their memories of the circumstances of the robbery. Most importantly, the witness will doubt themselves when identifying the robbers, and the latter will get a real chance at avoiding punishment.

Both condemning and exonerative evidence can be erroneous. The annals of the justice system are filled with miscarriages of justice, where false memories led to guilty verdicts for innocent people. Children's testimonies are especially suspect. Strong imaginations and high suggestibility make them poor witnesses.

Memory is not a data storehouse, but is built via the process of its reconstruction. External intervention in this process influences the result. Not only can you change or destroy existing memories, you can introduce new ones. Experiments show that in about 30% of cases, adult subjects can be made to falsely recall memories of childhood. In some cases, these memories begin living in their own lives: they become fleshed out, vivid and emotional.

False memories of events in adulthood can also be planted, especially if a lie is mixed with the truth. Sometimes the ability to 'remind' someone about a non-existent event helps intelligence officers, especially those functioning outside the law.

Successful suggestion of adulthood memories can require more work. There are some tips for this below:

1. A lot of time must pass after the event. To plant the memory of an event that did not take place, it is necessary for it to have 'happened' three to five years ago. To suggest details of actual events, the time frame can be reduced to a few months.

2. The description of the event must be believable. Lies must be mixed with the truth. Be sure to tie a non-existent event with other, real, scenes from a person's life.

3. The story will be more convincing if it contains a lot of details.

4. The story is easier to believe if it contains information from the different senses: images, sounds and smells.

5. It is best to support your story with fraudulent documents photographs or the testimony of authoritative witnesses.

6. Introducing false memories takes time. There should be breaks between 'suggestion sessions' so the information can get fixed in the subject's memory. Even if a person denies everything at first, in the time between, they will start to doubt. This will create a basis for consequent 'sessions'. It will be necessary to revisit the memory several times: the more repetitions the person hears, the more firmly the suggestion will take hold.

7. In case of rejection, your strategy should focus on the unreliability of memory: 'Please try to remember', 'You're just forgetting, that's not what happened', 'That can't be, because . . .' etc. Leading questions formulated so that they already contain the correct answer can also help: 'Didn't he have a beard?' 'It was evening. Remember, the streetlights were on?'

Memory manipulation can be completely innocent – 'Santa brought you a gift!' Or it can be very dangerous: political propaganda often lies, trying to rewrite the history of a country – the collective memory of its citizens.

Exercise

Plant a false memory into the mind of one of your acquaintances. For example, a funny or awkward situation that arose at a party. Make up a detailed story and a strategy for its suggestion. Prepare 'witnesses' and 'material evidence', if possible. Do not give up after the first rejection.

Ask your target to remember and to give you more details. Perhaps the story will be more colourful and interesting than you thought at first.

Be careful: implanting false memories on subjects can injure the psyche. As soon as your acquaintance believes you, admit that you have been playing a prank.

Lie detector

A polygraph (popularly referred to as a lie detector) is a device that measures and records information on the physiological state of a person: pulse, blood pressure, respiration, galvanic skin response, muscle tension, trembling of the limbs, etc.

When telling a lie, a person enters into an internal conflict. They feel guilty and afraid that the truth will come out, and they will be punished. Internal conflict generates strong emotions that are easily seen on a polygraph. However, the polygraph does not detect lies directly, it only shows emotional excitement that, when properly interpreted, indicates that the subject is lying.

Ninety per cent of the result of polygraph testing depends on the knowledge and experience of the operator. First, the reaction depends on the asked questions. They should be well prepared and arranged in the right order. Second, the operator needs to understand how a lie shows up in the emotional reactions of the individual. After all, the subject can be worried even when telling the truth because of the fear of the testing procedure itself.

The operator makes the final decision on whether the subject is telling the truth or a lie, and it is subjective in many ways. In interpreting physiological indicators, an operator risks committing one of two errors: declaring a false testimony true or accusing an honest subject of lying. The quality of a polygraph test strongly depends on the questions asked. There are two types of questions: relevant and control. The first type of question is directly related to the testing goal. The second type helps to understand what happens to the subject when they lie. Control questions are chosen so that the subject is forced to lie to keep up their reputation.

For example, a relevant question can be: 'Have you given classified information to unauthorized parties?' and a control question: 'Have you ever appropriated other people's belongings?' Typically, a person has taken someone else's belongings at least once. However, not wanting to look like a thief, they are likely to lie about it. This will trigger an emotional response, which is necessary for an analysis of the reaction to a relevant question.

Due to the fact that emotions are individual, an operator does not interpret reactions themselves but the difference between them. If the relevant question causes a stronger response than the control one, the subject is more likely to be afraid of being incriminated. If the other way round, like most people, they are concerned about keeping up his or her reputation and the charge of espionage will appear unsubstantiated.

Polygraphs can be cheated and good intelligence officers know how to do it. There are so many ways to pass the test that experts have combined them into groups.

1. Mechanical methods are the simplest. You need to cause pain, biting the tongue or the cheek, bending your toes down hard or pushing them into a pin in your shoe.

Pain and muscle tension distort physiological parameters, making it difficult for the operator to work. However, experienced examiners notice mechanical resistance during testing, and this will not play in the favour of the subject.

2. Pharmacological methods. Taking a sedative or stimulant distorts the figures that the examiner uses as a base to distinguish truth from lies. You should be careful when using this method: the use of psychoactive substances can be betrayed by the narrowing or dilation of pupils, or a change in pulse or skin colour. Furthermore, there is a risk of overdose.

3. Behavioural methods: inappropriate friendliness, chit-chat with the examiner, repeating questions, silliness. Excessive excitement distorts physiological indicators. If falsehood is indicated by the difference in response to relevant and control questions, it can be ironed out with enhanced responses on all questions or any other things the examiner says. Excessively familiar or relaxed behaviour also makes the examiner's job more difficult.

4. Mental methods are a group of techniques based on psychological self-regulation. This group includes relaxation techniques borrowed from yoga and other Eastern practices, and forms of distraction as complicated as mental calculations or enhanced reflection on any problem. This group of methods is very effective, but requires serious preparation.

The rationalization method also works well. Knowing the purpose of the test, a person prepares for it ahead of time. In order not to show anxiety and excitement on relevant questions, they plant in their own mind a rational explanation of the act that they want to hide. For example, giving classified information to a foreign intelligence officer can be reinterpreted as dissemination of scientific information that is no longer confidential and should be used for peaceful purposes. A store clerk can convince himself that he acted justly: he took what he was owed because he was underpaid, and did not steal anything. Properly designed rationalization is very effective as it gives a person confidence in his or her actions and resolves the internal conflict caused by a lie. For this reason false memories cannot be recognized with a polygraph: the person being tested is absolutely convinced they are true.

There is no thoroughly reliable method of deceiving a polygraph, as there is no absolutely accurate way of interpreting physiological indicators. But passing a lie detector requires knowledge and training.

Exercise

Learn to manage your physiological indicators. You will need a pulse or galvanic skin resistance sensor. These are placed on the fingers or earlobes, and when connected to a monitor allow you to track physiological parameters in real time.

There are many computer programs that help you learn to consciously manage your physiological state. This skill will be useful for more than just polygraph tests.

★ Train your brain – Opposites

Look at the table below. In this exercise, you need to say out loud the opposite of the words in the squares, ignoring what is written down on the page. For example, if you see the word 'light', you should say the word 'dark'. Continue to repeat this exercise to increase perception and mental agility.

big	cheap	clean	deep	down	early	easy
full	good	happy	heavy	here	high	hot
light	long	loud	many	new	rich	right
safe	soft	strong	tall	thick	warm	wet
wife	young	smooth	inter-esting	outside	rough	smooth
fat	fast	far	wide	bold	scared	sit

You've come a long way. You've spent a lot of time training. Undoubtedly, your memory has improved. In addition, you've also improved your ability to work with information, organize your time and communicate with people. Do not stop here. Come back to exercises from the book. Limit the use of electronic devices and load your memory. This is how you can maintain and enhance your mental abilities.

In addition to the techniques needed to work with information, this book has described methods of communicating with people used by the intelligence services. Some of them can cause harm – be very careful when using them.

←

How much can you remember?

Alvarez-Finke was sentenced to twenty-five years in
prison. He died in prison.

A. N. Simonov, 'Simonides', became an analyst in the
Second Main Directorate. He married a colleague.
An attempt to recruit Simonov was made by foreign
intelligence. With the authorities' approval he
agreed, and through him a double game was played for
a long time.

François Legly became a diplomat and died in Algeria
in 1961.

As of this date, RSHA documents have not been
declassified. Kovalev's thesis was finished by another
student, who narrowed the topic down to the use of
Schultz's autogenic training.

Bernstein was never found.

— —

Answers – Test yourself

p.13   B)

p.17   C)

p.29   B)

p.38   B)

p.42   B)

p.53   A), C), D) and E)

p.73   B)

p.83   B)

p.103   D)

p.124   Archeologist, Michael and Rostovets

p.140   C)

p.149   B)

p.166   C)

p.183   B) and C)

p.202   C)

p.214   B) and C)

p.225   A)

p.243   B) and F)

p.251   D)

Acknowledgements for the Russian edition

This book came into being thanks to quite a few people.

Concept, text and illustrations for Simonides's journal – Denis Bukin.

Authorized translation – Svetlana Shcholokova. Editing, Simonides's journal – Vladimir Vdovikov. Copyediting of the English text – Alexandra Kollontai. Photographs – Kamil Guliev.

Illustrations – Vasiliy Yaltonskiy.

Interactive exercises – Natalia Kuznetsova, Pavel Kabir, Ilya Zubarev, Sergei Zudin, Galina Smirnova.

Layout – Lesya Kovtun, Denis Burin.

Website, www.improve-memory.net – Rustem Razmanov, Sergei Zudin.

We would like to thank:

Katya Grebneva for participating in discussions, for her help and understanding, and also for proofreading the electronic version of the book.

Svetlana Shcholokova for contributing to developing the concept for the book and her many suggestions.

Vladimir Vdovikov for his editorial thoroughness.

Alexandra Kollontai for her creative contribution to the entire English text of the book.

Irina Guskina for her cooperation and support.

Lesya Kovtun, Oksana Tretyakov, Valentin Lapchevskiy for their work on the design and presentation of the book.

Models: Artem Petrosov, Vladimir Ipatov, Vladimir Maltsev, Ivan Pronchev, Margarita Krinochkina, Vasiliy Afanasyev, Natalia Kuznetsova, Elizaveta Lapteva, Nikolai Sergeyev, Oksana Tretyakova, Valentin Lapchevskiy, Elena Markova, Svetlana Shcholokova, Anastasia Egorova, Alyona Gok, Anton Iskrin, Tatiana Shiryayeva.

Sergei Plohov and Maxim Aleshin for contributing specialized props.

Friends for clothing and accessories for shoots.

Bayram Annakov and the entire Empatika team for believing in the project.

Thank you to Olga Labutina for her support and warm, friendly participation.